ASSESSMENT as a *Catalyst* for LEARNING

Creating a Responsive and Fluid Process
to Inspire All Students

Garnet Hillman
Mandy Stalets

Solution Tree | Press

a division of
Solution Tree

555 North Morton Street
Bloomington, IN 47404
800.733.6786 (toll free) / 812.336.7700
FAX: 812.336.7790

email: info@SolutionTree.com
SolutionTree.com

Visit **go.SolutionTree.com/assessment** to download the free reproducibles in this book.

Printed in the United States of America

Library of Congress Cataloging-in-Publication Data

Names: Hillman, Garnet, author. | Stalets, Mandy, author.
Title: Assessment as a catalyst for learning : creating a responsive and
  fluid process to inspire all students / Garnet Hillman, Mandy Stalets.
Description: Bloomington, IN : Solution Tree Press, 2022. | Includes
  bibliographical references and index.
Identifiers: LCCN 2021014257 (print) | LCCN 2021014258 (ebook) | ISBN
  9781952812231 (paperback) | ISBN 9781952812248 (ebook)
Subjects: LCSH: Educational tests and measurements. | Motivation in
  education. | Effective teaching.
Classification: LCC LB3051 .H533 2022 (print) | LCC LB3051 (ebook) | DDC
  371.26--dc23
LC record available at https://lccn.loc.gov/2021014257
LC ebook record available at https://lccn.loc.gov/2021014258

Solution Tree
Jeffrey C. Jones, CEO
Edmund M. Ackerman, President

Solution Tree Press
President and Publisher: Douglas M. Rife
Associate Publisher: Sarah Payne-Mills
Art Director: Rian Anderson
Managing Production Editor: Kendra Slayton
Copy Chief: Jessi Finn
Production Editor: Miranda Addonizio
Content Development Specialist: Amy Rubenstein
Copy Editor: Jessi Finn
Proofreader: Sarah Ludwig
Text and Cover Designer: Kelsey Hergül
Editorial Assistants: Sarah Ludwig and Elijah Oates

Acknowledgments

This book is dedicated to the educator who had an a-ha moment and said, "Assessment is learning!" during a workshop. This occurrence inspired this book and frames the professional development we deliver surrounding the topic of assessment.

Garnet would like to thank her husband, Shawn, and sons, Julian and Jackson, for their patience and support throughout the writing of this book. Their varied perspectives on learning provide an essential window into how assessment is perceived by students and adults alike.

Mandy would like to thank her husband, Luke, and daughters, Eva and Alex, for their never-ending support and patience as she wrote this book and taught during the pandemic. Thanks for always allowing me to put one more thing on my plate, and then helping me balance it all.

Solution Tree Press would like to thank the following reviewers:

Charles Ames Fischer
Education Consultant
Decatur, Tennessee

Laura Liccione
Coordinator of Academic
 Improvement
Baltimore, Maryland

Eric Lindblad
English Teacher

Andover High School
Andover, Minnesota

Nicole McRee
Science Instructional Coach
Kildeer Countryside District 96
Buffalo Grove, Illinois

Lauren Smith
Instructional Coach
Noble Crossing Elementary School,

Visit **go.SolutionTree.com/assessment** to download the free reproducibles in this book.

Table of Contents

Reproducibles are in italics.

About the Authors

 **Garnet Hillman** is an educator, author, presenter, and learner. She has served as an instructional coach at Caruso Middle School and as a Spanish teacher at Lockport Township High School, both in Illinois. She consults around the United States on the topics of assessment, grading, and student motivation. A passionate educator, Garnet values student learning above all else.

Through her consulting work, Garnet emphasizes healthy grading and sound assessment practices. She has worked with a variety of school districts that desire to improve instruction, provide relevant and respectful assessment, cultivate grading practices that support learning, and increase student motivation. She provides rationale for a paradigm shift in grading methods and a practical, step-by-step process to implement the change. She is the coauthor of the books *Standards-Based Learning in Action: Moving From Theory to Practice*, *The Grade Cleanse*, *Coaching Your Classroom: How to Deliver Actionable Feedback to Students*, and *Moving Beyond Classroom Management: Leading a Culture of Learning*.

Garnet holds a master's degree in educational leadership from Aurora University, as well as a bachelor's degree in Spanish from Ohio University. She has also completed graduate coursework in instructional technology.

To learn more about Garnet Hillman's work, follow @garnet_hillman on Twitter.

Mandy Stalets works with a wide variety of teachers, undergraduate students, and school districts to improve assessment and grading practices to maximize communication and student success. She provides rationale for the need for change in our current grading practices, as well as practical steps for implementation. Mandy is a teacher and learner who is passionate about sound assessment and grading practices, as well as standards-based learning. Along with her consulting work, she is currently a high school mathematics teacher at Illinois State University's laboratory schools. She is also the co-moderator of Solution Tree's assessment Twitter chat, #ATAssessment, and coauthor of the books *Standards-Based Learning in Action: Moving From Theory to Practice* and *Coaching Your Classroom: How to Deliver Actionable Feedback to Students.*

Mandy received her undergraduate degree in secondary mathematics education and graduate degree in teaching and learning from Illinois State University. She received her National Board Certification in Early Adolescence Mathematics in 2017.

To learn more about Mandy Stalets's work, follow @MandyStalets on Twitter.

To book Garnet Hillman or Mandy Stalets for professional development, contact pd@SolutionTree.com.

Introduction

Assessment occupies such a central position in good teaching because we cannot predict what students will learn.

—Dylan Wiliam

As we talked about writing this book, we spent a significant amount of time discussing our own experience (or lack thereof) with learning about assessment. Assessment literacy wasn't a focal point in our college experiences or early years in the classroom. While we are now both experienced teachers and writers in the area of assessment, neither of us had any formal training on how to *use* assessment to increase student hope, motivation, and learning as we embarked on our careers. Without this training, we both started teaching using assessment in the way our teachers used it on us—as a way to quantify learning on a chosen arbitrary date.

During the creation of this book, we discussed how we were never taught how to design or use assessment in a way that inspired learning. We questioned why it is that K–12 education has traditionally framed assessment as a punishment or sorting mechanism instead of a way to inspire and teach students. Even in our travels and extensive work with schools as educational consultants, we often hear the same idea that teachers have not received adequate training in how to *use* assessment to empower students and increase learning. Assessment is too often an afterthought instead of a forethought that drives instruction and identifies needs along the way. Assessment is too often a method to punish students for not learning fast enough rather than a tool to identify where they are and help show them the way forward. It is time to change the dialogue around assessment to ensure that assessment is a learning experience for all.

Assessment has long been an integral part of the educational system, but a growing body of research, which we will unpack in this book, points to the fact that assessment, when used in the appropriate manner, has a profound and lasting influence on student learning and efficacy. While assessment *for* learning (teachers use evidence from assessment to inform their teaching) and assessment *of* learning (teachers use evidence of student learning against standards to judge proficiency) have become common language in the 21st century classroom, this book stretches those thoughts to assert that assessment *is* learning—a catalyst. We should think of assessment not as its noun form but rather as a verb, *assess*—an action word that encompasses the means of observing, collecting data, and responding based on what the student needs. This might involve throwing some well-structured plans out the window in favor of *in-the-moment* reactions and responses, but teachers can center these on one critical element—support that students *need* at this juncture in order to learn. Assessing in this manner will increase hope and inspire learning. In service of this mindset shift, in the following sections, we explain how assessment is a process and then go into further detail about what you can expect as you read this book.

The Assessment Process

This book outlines assessment not as an event but as a process by which teachers can increase learning both for themselves and their teams as well as for their students. Just as a catalyst can bring about change, sound assessment practices transform the learning experience. Assessment *is* learning when students understand their learning objectives and can take an active role in monitoring their own progress. Assessment *is* learning when students can design their own path to proficiency with the guidance of a teacher and when feedback and coaching play an integral role in the learning process. Assessment *is* learning when teachers and students view it not as a punitive practice but as an instructional support that promotes students' growth.

Figure I.1 provides a structure of the assessment process for the classroom teacher or teacher team looking to create a more student-centered learning experience. Aligned with the work of Grant Wiggins and Jay McTighe (1998, 2005) in *Understanding by Design*, this backward design of assessment allows teachers to engage in instruction with a clear picture of what students will be learning and the intended rigor. It also gives teachers clear steps for using ongoing assessment to keep students well informed of their progress and coach them forward. By intentionally designing the final destination, teachers can be more mindful and intentional in their design of assessment and instruction. By engaging in this process as a team, teachers collectively understand intended outcomes and how assessment supports learning along the way. This ensures an equitable learning experience for students.

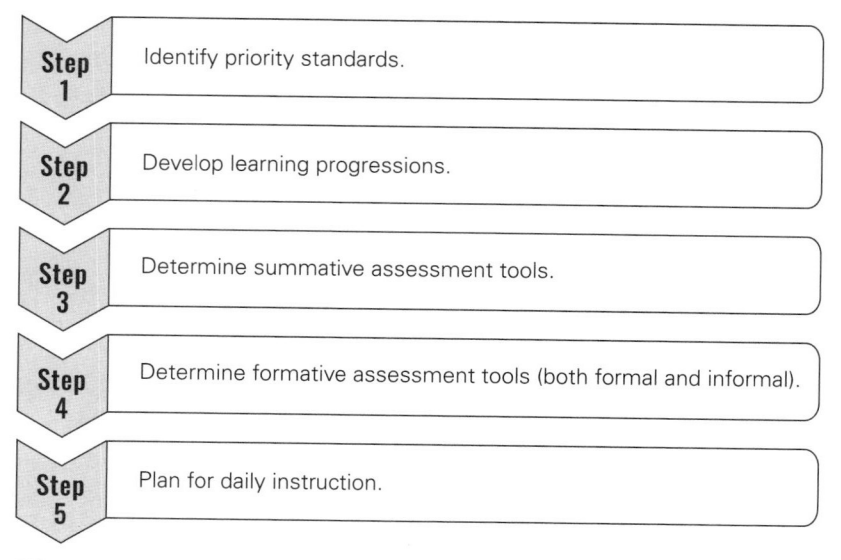

Step 1 | Identify priority standards.

Step 2 | Develop learning progressions.

Step 3 | Determine summative assessment tools.

Step 4 | Determine formative assessment tools (both formal and informal).

Step 5 | Plan for daily instruction.

FIGURE I.1: Assessment process.

The following is a brief description of each step in the process. After chapter 1, in which we discuss how teachers and teams can define and come to a shared understanding of the different types of assessment, we unpack each of these steps in much further detail.

Step 1: Identify Priority Standards

To begin a journey, you need a destination. For the assessment process, this destination keeps plans for assessment grounded and centered on specific learning intentions. Identifying priority standards for each unit or period of time in advance of any instruction is essential in order to display a clear goal for both teachers and learners. As outlined in chapter 2, this allows teachers or teams to determine the *essential* and non-negotiable outcomes (priority standards) that the students should be proficient with at the end of the period of learning. Identifying these standards as a first step dictates the destination so that teachers can plan the journey.

Step 2: Develop Learning Progressions

Standards contain highly sophisticated language that will often be too complex for a learner to fully comprehend from the outset of a unit. The technical jargon and combination of many skills and contexts may even present challenges to the expert classroom teacher. Thus, the next step after determining priority standards is to break down those large standards into small, digestible pieces (learning targets) and place the targets into a natural sequence of learning (learning progression—addressed in chapter 2) that shows the steps students will take through learning. For teachers and teacher teams, this provides a road map and communicates how their teaching and support for students will advance throughout the learning process. For students, progressions provide a transparent outline of their learning and expectations.

Step 3: Determine Summative Assessment Tools

Next, teachers must create tools to use for summative assessment (explored in chapter 3) so they can ensure that all teachers understand what proficiency with the standards will look like and how they will expect students to showcase that proficiency. Creating the summative tool prior to beginning a unit of study does not mean teachers are *teaching to the test*. It means teachers have a clear and shared vision (if working in teams) of proficiency with the skills, the products students are expected to create, and the end goal for learning. Within teams, summative assessment tools do not need to be the same. However, the evidence students are asked to produce, no matter the assessment tool, must meet the demands of the standards. With the end goal in mind, teachers allow themselves more focused flexibility as they move through instruction.

Step 4: Determine Formative Assessment Tools (Informal and Formal)

Once the destination is set, teachers can decide how to mindfully monitor learning to collect data and respond based on the emerging, in-the-moment needs of their learners. Chapters 4 and 5 will look at informal formative versus formal formative assessment. *Informal formative assessment* refers to the on-the-spot decisions that teachers use to engage in instructional agility and pivot based on emerging evidence of learning. *Formal formative assessment* refers to the more obtrusive, planned formative assessments that teachers use to make instructional decisions and align to the learning progressions in advance of instruction. A way we have often found helpful to indicate the distinction is to present informal formative assessment with a lowercase *f* and formal Formative assessment with an uppercase *F*.

Teachers and teacher teams intentionally place informal and formal formative assessments within instruction to check progress on skills that are difficult to learn, hard to teach, and worthy of intervention and enrichment. Informal formative assessment is planned by individual teachers to meet the needs of their learners while formal formative assessment can be a shared experience for teams when planning units of study. This allows teachers to preplan data collection points throughout the unit that will reveal how students are doing, and in turn, use those data to inform their instruction. These checkpoints are intended not to punish students but to personalize the learning process and give students the feedback and instruction they need to be more successful.

Step 5: Plan for Daily Instruction

The design of daily instruction (the focus of chapter 6) must be the last step in planning if teachers want to have a student-centered classroom that meets the needs of learners. Responsive teaching will vary from classroom to classroom to ensure the needs of all students are met. Teachers must use ongoing formative assessment evidence and data to plan daily instruction. If they set daily lesson plans before assessing, the content and tasks, rather than student needs, are driving the classroom experience. At this step in the assessment process, formative data allow teachers to understand what students know and need so that they may plan accordingly.

About This Book

This book takes a deep dive into outlining the learning associated with the assessment process for educators and students. We frame the discussion with research while offering practical steps for application, which apply for both individual teachers and teams looking to improve assessment practices. Our suggestions will work well for any team, including collaborative teams within professional learning communities (PLCs). Each chapter is organized into the following sections.

- **What Is It?** This section defines the different pieces of the assessment process and highlights how teachers can use them in the classroom.

- **Learning for Teachers:** This section focuses on the specific learning for classroom teachers that happens with a particular part of the assessment process.

- **Learning for Students:** This section makes apparent for teachers the moments when their students can learn more about who they are, how they learn, and how they can move forward with their skills and proficiency during the assessment process.

- **Collaboration Around Assessment:** This section dives into the use of assessment as part of a collaborative teacher team. Collaborative teams can use the process provided by the four critical questions and three big ideas of a PLC (DuFour, DuFour, Eaker, Many, & Mattos, 2016) to ensure that team time spent discussing assessment is worthwhile and productive. This collaboration surrounding assessment moves learning forward for teachers by bringing together multiple perspectives and increased resources.

- **Questions for Reflection:** This list of questions provides thought-provoking opportunities to reflect and look forward in any individual teacher or teacher team's assessment journey.

- **Next Steps for Implementation:** This reproducible tool is a flowchart for educators to use as they engage in the chapter's highlighted aspect of the assessment process.

A learning process that uses assessment as a catalyst keeps our most critical stakeholders (learners) as the driving force behind all instructional decisions. When teachers assess as part of the classroom experience, learning becomes a responsive and fluid process. When assessment is an embedded part of the learning experience, it is done *with* students, not *to* students. They are supported through their learning rather than penalized for their mistakes. Assessment *is* learning.

chapter one

ASSESSMENT DEFINED

Assessment is the engine
that drives student learning.

—*John Cowan*

Assessment is a learning process for everyone in the classroom. From the determination of standards, targets, and progressions before units begin, to the summative process, from the formative process to instruction, assessment guides learning. Each assessment should not simply be a judge of student understanding; it should be a springboard to continue learning. When teachers use assessment in a way that aligns with its intended purpose, students will learn while engaging in the process.

It is crucial that all members of a school, individuals and teacher teams alike, have the same understanding of how assessment is defined, as well as the role assessment plays in the learning process. This chapter highlights the importance of a solid and shared understanding of the definition and purpose of assessment. This understanding may start with individual teachers, but it is imperative that this cultural shift is school- or districtwide if the hope is to impact learning for all students.

What Is It?

The word *assessment* often conjures up images or memories of events such as quizzes, tests, exit tickets, and projects, as well as feelings of angst or worry from fear of judgment or failure due to past assessment experiences. While those images and those feelings are valid, they do not represent what assessment could and should be *today*. For too many years, assessment has been something that teachers do *to* learners, instead of *with* learners; it has punished students for the absence of a skill instead of providing the feedback and support necessary for them to acquire that skill.

Traditionally, assessments have become disjointed events instead of a process that students value because it empowers them and provides information they need in order to grow and improve. The word *assessment* is not synonymous with a certain task type such as a test or project. Assessment (when used appropriately) is the most powerful tool that both teachers and learners possess to improve learning.

We wrote this chapter with the intent to redefine assessment, both formative and summative, and its use in the everyday classroom to support and maximize learning for both teachers and learners. We'll start by further explaining the process of assessment and then present and discuss some fundamental truths about assessment. After that, we'll explicitly define formative and summative assessment before discussing how this clarity informs a healthy culture of assessment, how the two types of assessment are interdependent, and how they can work in a digital world.

The Process of Assessment

The process of assessment starts with planning. Teachers first consider the question, What do students need to know and be able to do? and then move to the question, How will we know when they have learned it? in order to establish a shared understanding for themselves and a clear goal for students (DuFour, DuFour, Eaker, & Many, 2010; DuFour et al., 2016). Teacher- and team-level conversations then look at strategic checkpoints along the way to that learning goal and possible interventions that will support students who need more instruction and enrichment for those who show early proficiency. This procedure keeps student learning at the center and uses assessment as the primary source of information.

The purpose of assessment is to gather the information necessary to personalize the learning process and maximize growth. Assessment should not be used to sort or punish but instead be used to inspire learning for both teachers and students. Through sound, student-centered assessment practices, teachers should be able to answer the following questions.

- What will the student learn from this assessment?

- What will I learn from this assessment about my own instruction?

- What can I learn about the learning styles of my students so that I can improve?

- What will tomorrow look like based on the evidence I see today?

- What can my collaborative team learn from the assessment process?

When teachers view assessment through the lens of learning, not evaluating, it opens the door to expand understanding of not only student learning and instruction but also the development of assessment practices. This increases teachers' capacity to learn about their students and allows assessment to be an invitation to a collaborative conversation of learning.

Research through the years has found that frequent formative assessments have a greater impact on student learning than infrequent assessments (Bangert-Drowns, Kulik, & Kulik, 1991; Fuchs & Fuchs, 1986; Lee, 2006; Marzano, 2017). When teachers infuse formative assessment into everyday instruction and students consistently get feedback on their progress, assessment becomes essential to the learning process and fuels growth.

For the teacher, assessment is a chance to get to know the needs, strengths, and learning styles of all students in order to create a more differentiated and impactful classroom. For students, assessment is a chance to show what they have learned so that the teacher can design learning pathways to coach each individual forward.

Assessment Truths

All educators must understand and be able to apply sound assessment practices if they hope to maximize learning. Meaningful assessment is not possible unless educators understand how to use it to positively impact student learning. The following are five truths and non-negotiables when it comes to implementing sound assessment practices, whether at the classroom, school, or district level.

1. Assessment drives learning and instruction.

2. Assessment informs learning and instruction.

3. Assessment informs students of their progress.

4. Assessment informs teachers of what comes next.

5. Assessment informs teachers of immediate needs.

We'll discuss each of these in more detail in the following sections.

Assessment Drives Learning and Instruction

Learning is not a straight path but a messy and tangled journey, especially when considering all the different readiness levels and learning styles present within the walls of one classroom. Teachers must carefully consider both students' readiness levels and their diverse learning styles before embarking on new learning. When approaching a new unit, teachers need to collect evidence and data (whether formal or informal) on what learners know or do not know to determine their own entry point with new instruction. Teachers can use assessment to ensure that they are meeting their students' needs and readiness for new learning. Through assessment, teachers have the ability to see where learning journeys *begin* and can adjust accordingly.

Consider a high school algebra class starting a new unit of study. This unit will require some prerequisite skills for students to successfully engage with their new learning. The new skill in this unit has students solving systems of linear equations. To begin, students need to have a good understanding of slope and graphing lines in slope-intercept form. If the teacher assumes that this prerequisite knowledge is present when it is not, students could be attempting to learn a new skill while at the same time filling in gaps with prior skills that they have not yet mastered.

As the teacher begins this unit of study, he recognizes that students will come in at various levels and wants to spend time intervening where necessary. On the first day of the unit, he brings in graphing marker boards. The class begins with a student-driven discussion about what they remember about graphing linear equations. Students talk about the slope formula, slope-intercept form of a line, and rise over run as well as intercepts of a graph. The teacher then transitions and asks students to use the marker boards to graph different lines. During these formative activities, the teacher actively notices students who are struggling or resistant to engage. The teacher uses the observations to form strategic groupings for the next day to reach students who do not possess the prerequisite skills. Throughout this lesson, the teacher is using assessment to drive learning and instruction.

Assessment Informs Learning and Instruction

While this truth might sound similar to the first assessment truth, this one is about adapting *within* the learning process of acquiring a new skill. While being able to teach in a logical progression with a new topic every day sounds ideal, it is far from the reality of 21st century classrooms. Learners' needs vary from day to day; thus, instruction needs to follow suit. Teachers' response to assessment data in the form of feedback, coaching, and responsive and targeted instruction informs the student of future learning (Hillman & Stalets, 2019).

As an example, think of a middle school team of four language arts teachers who have created a common formative assessment to address whether students can identify a theme. They have planned to administer this assessment after three days of instruction and practice. After giving the assessment, the collaborative team analyzes its data and notices that there are twenty students across the four teachers who are not yet proficient with this skill. Because of this, the teachers collaboratively discuss strategic interventions for those students as well as enrichment opportunities for the rest of the learners. They then share resources that they can use the following day to meet the needs of all their students. Assessment within the process of learning informs student-centered decisions about next steps.

Assessment Informs Students of Their Progress

Learning should never be a guessing game for students. Once teachers have deconstructed standards and put them in students' hands, students should be able to map and measure their own progress through learning. Students' ownership of their own learning is key; "student investment occurs when assessment and self-regulation have a symbiotic relationship" (Erkens, Schimmer, & Dimich, 2017, p. 112). Whether they are kindergarten students or high school seniors, learners should be able to measure and see their own progress.

Consider a scenario in which a kindergarten student is sharing her learning with her parents. The student comes home, opens her reading folder, and is excited to show off several pieces of paper that display letters of the alphabet. She grabs the paper at the top of the pile, which has a few letters highlighted in blue, and says, "These were the letters I knew on the first day of school." She then flips to the next page; this one has quite a few more letters highlighted, this time in green, and she explains that after a couple of weeks of school, she had learned so many more letters! She flips through a couple more pages until she gets to the last one, where all the letters are colored, and she says, "I did it! I learned them all! I got to take these papers out of my data notebook and bring them home so that I can show you!" Her excitement is contagious as she shows and communicates her progress. When her parents ask if she is also able to identify the capital letters, she says, "Almost. I only have five left!" and names what those letters are. Even at a young age, this learner knows what she knows, what she does not know, and what comes next. She is even excited to show and celebrate her growth.

Assessment Informs Teachers of What Comes Next

Teachers must pair effective assessment practices with meaningful feedback meant to coach all learners forward and make them active participants in the learning process. John Hattie and Helen Timperley (2007) explain that feedback should answer three questions: (1) Where am I going? (2) How am I going? and (3) Where to next? These questions align with D. Royce Sadler's (1989) three questions: (1) Where am I going? (2) Where am I now? and (3) How do I close the gap? Keeping focus on these questions allows teachers to meet students where they are and lead them to what comes next while reaching for student self-awareness and ownership. It is essential that effective assessment stimulates thinking (Wiliam, 2013) and, as Hattie and Timperley (2007) outline, answers the question, What next? Feedback that looks forward keeps both teacher and learner focused on growth and next steps.

Think about a fifth-grade student who is working on a project for science. This project asks students to create a model to describe how the energy in an animal's food comes from the sun. The teacher has developed a feedback routine where each student receives recognition of a strength, information about an area that needs strengthening, and a brief description of what comes next. This student's feedback indicates that a clear description of an animal's food is present, but the connection to the sun is missing. It also provides a resource the student can use to learn more about this connection. The teacher devotes the first few minutes of work the next day to reading and preparing to respond to the feedback. She reminds students to look for explicit information in their feedback that describes next steps to improve their work. Students receive time to collaborate and improve before resubmitting their work to the teacher. The fifth-grade student is now empowered to gather information from that resource to further develop her project. This assessment process informs students of what comes next and gives them time to take action.

Assessment Informs Teachers of Immediate Needs

Because of this truth, teachers must constantly observe and collect data on the class's needs in order to quickly adjust their instruction based on emerging evidence. The word *immediate* reiterates the fact that assessment is not an event but a process. Formative assessment for the purpose of determining immediate needs could come in the form of conversations, observations, think-pair-shares, turn-and-talks, or other unobtrusive classroom activities. (We will cover this type of formative assessment in more detail in chapter 4, page 73.) The critical elements are that teachers keep the end goal in mind and they are comfortable being agile in their instruction based on these classroom observations and formative data. Reflecting on the previous examples of the assessment truths, notice that each time the teacher is using the data in a formative manner. There is a focus on feedback, student ownership and response, and teacher agility to address student needs. Assessment should inform teachers of their next steps to maximize learning.

Let's take a moment to make sure we are clear on how formative assessment differs from summative assessment.

Definitions of Formative and Summative Assessment

Assessment in the classroom setting generally falls into three categories: (1) preassessment (assessment to determine readiness), (2) formative assessment (assessment to inform next steps), and (3) summative assessment (assessment to verify learning). Preassessment can be considered as a part of the formative paradigm because its use guides decisions about future teaching and learning. Assessment should not be defined by its timing, title, or task type; it should be defined by the type of evidence gathered and the instructional response to the collected data. An assessment should not be labeled formative just because it occurs in the middle of learning. Instead, what makes an assessment formative in nature is the instructional response to the data collected from learners. What makes an assessment summative is the collection of data to verify that learning has occurred.

The distinction between formative and summative assessment is not simply a determination as to whether to assign a grade to the work. The distinction lies in whether the teacher will use the data to guide student learning as a checkpoint or the teacher will use the data to determine proficiency. The same assessment can be used formatively (to instructionally respond to meet learners' needs) or summatively (to record learners' proficiency). A teacher might intend to use an assessment for the purpose of summative evaluation but might instead use it formatively if students do not display an adequate level of proficiency. Table 1.1 outlines some characteristics of formative and summative assessments and their uses in the classroom.

TABLE 1.1: *Characteristics of Formative and Summative Assessment*

CHARACTERISTICS OF FORMATIVE ASSESSMENT	CHARACTERISTICS OF SUMMATIVE ASSESSMENT
· Provides robust data that allow for an instructional response · Informs students of what comes next on their personal learning journey · Allows for feedback that is actionable in nature · Has the potential to have a profound and lasting influence on student learning · Is infused into everyday instruction to allow for agility on the part of the teacher	· Guides the reporting process · Confirms students' proficiency level · Occurs after students have had ample time to practice and develop proficiency · Can also become formative in nature with an instructional response

It can also be argued that every assessment event can be labeled as formative if the teacher is constantly revising and adapting instruction and practice based on emerging learner evidence. The event does not dictate the response; every assessment event is an opportunity for everyone involved to learn and grow.

Research continues to show that formative assessment has a positive effect on student learning (Chappuis & Stiggins, 2020; Chappuis, Stiggins, Chappuis, & Arter,

2012; Heritage, 2008; Organisation for Economic Co-operation and Development, 2005; Popham, 2008; Wiliam, 2018). Through their extensive research, Paul Black and Dylan Wiliam (1998a) describe that formative assessment is "amongst the largest ever reported for educational interventions" (p. 61). That is, formative assessment plays one of the largest roles in advancing student learning.

Formative assessment holds the promise that teachers and learners go through the learning journey together. The non-negotiable element is that teachers must pair formative assessment with an instructional response to see increased achievement. A quick internet search of the word *formative* (n.d.) produces the following definition: "serving to form something, especially having a profound and lasting influence on a person's development." The term *assessment* comes from the Latin root *assidere*, which means "to sit beside" (Slattery, 2018). When put together, *formative assessment* should be an experience where a teacher works alongside students to have a profound and lasting influence on their learning. The formative process should not quantify learning while students are still in the process of improving. It should give feedback, form a partnership between teacher and learner, and encourage continued growth and learning.

Here's an example to further clarify the difference between formative assessment and summative assessment. Imagine that a sixth-grade mathematics teacher gives students each an exit ticket on adding and subtracting fractions. He aligns this assessment to the intended standard and indicates to students that the assessment is formative. That night, the teacher takes the exit tickets (or the digital results) home and looks over student work. Let's consider two different scenarios of how the teacher might interact with the data: (1) using the assessment tool formatively and (2) using the assessment tool summatively.

Scenario 1: Using the Assessment Tool Formatively

When assigning the exit ticket, the teacher communicates to students that he plans to use this assessment formatively so he can target his instruction in the next couple of days to meet their needs. Thus, he encourages vulnerability and an understanding that their work should not be perfect—he must see what they know and what they need if he wants to plan accordingly.

When looking through the assessment results, the teacher searches for patterns. He finds that several students exhibit procedural fluency with the topic while several other students aren't quite understanding the concept of a common denominator. He decides to split the class's assessments into three groups: (1) students who need enrichment, (2) students who are close to the target and need a little more practice and guidance with manipulatives to truly understand common denominators, and

(3) students who require some reteaching of the content. When students enter the classroom the next day, they see their learning groups up on the board (predetermined by the teacher based on the formative results), and their warm-up tasks (designed to meet their groups' needs) are ready to go. The teacher knows he will stop by the group that needs reteaching first. He allows enough time during this warm-up to stop by each group, listen to its interactions, and respond accordingly.

In this scenario, the teacher chooses to use the assessment formatively. The data inform him of next steps and provide students with practice targeted to their needs. Notice that the teacher communicates the purpose of the assessment and then uses the data in a formative and targeted manner.

Scenario 2: Using the Assessment Tool Summatively

As the class is finishing its in-class work, the teacher makes an announcement that the students will wrap up five minutes early to take a formative assessment so that he can see how they are doing with the new content. That night, the teacher sits down with the students' exit tickets and grades them. He knows that the students are still in the process of learning and does not want to penalize them for early mistakes, so he keeps the assignment's point value low. He enters those scores into the online gradebook.

At the beginning of the next class period, the teacher returns the assessment results. He announces that he is making himself available to any students who have questions on their work after class and during their advisory period. That class period, the students start working with adding and subtracting mixed numbers. Notice that although the teacher calls the exit ticket a formative assessment, he does not use the data in a formative sense. Instead of responding to student needs in the moment, the primary purpose is judging proficiency and reporting. Student improvement cannot be expected without an instructional response.

Being clear about the assessment purpose allows students to view themselves as part of the assessment journey. This partnership provides a focus on growth and builds a positive, learner-centered classroom culture.

Culture of Assessment

Defining assessment, having a shared understanding of assessment's purposes, and communicating those purposes to students from the outset of a school year or course are critical elements to ensure students understand how to engage with assessment. Students must know that the teacher will use assessment as a stepping-stone to move them forward by gathering information about how they learn and what they learn.

This understanding opens the door to increased vulnerability and willingness to engage in the new content and skills. Defining assessment invites learners into the conversation and lets them know assessment is a tool that is there to support them as they move through learning. When students positively view assessment, it cultivates a positive culture.

Changing the way teachers and students communicate about assessment has the potential to help teachers evolve the classroom culture to focus on learning and growth. Consider the following language that teachers can use in the classroom when speaking about assessment to ease anxiety and allow students to be vulnerable throughout the learning process.

- **At the end of a class period:** "Before you leave, I need you to show me what you know. Please complete the problem on the board—wrong answers welcome—so that I can form groups to help you address any errors tomorrow."

- **Before administering a formal assessment:** "Since I am going to be providing you feedback on this assessment, I am going to ask you to provide me some feedback on this unit. How did it align with your learning style? Is there anything I could have done differently that would have helped you learn?"

- **Before administrating a formative assessment early in the learning process:** "Please remember that the purpose of assessment is for me to get information to best help you. If you get stuck, please ask questions. Write to me about where you get stuck and what you need so I can plan accordingly tomorrow and in future lessons."

- **After a student hands in work and communicates frustration:** "That's completely fine. We are still in the process of learning. I ask you to complete these assessments so that I get a look at what you don't know. I'll take a look at your work, and then I'd like to spend some one-on-one time with you tomorrow so we can go over what I see should come next for you."

Through each of these statements, teachers are communicating the purpose of the assessment and how the assessment is designed to support the learner. Assessment builds relationships, develops trust, teaches learners about learning styles, and allows for differentiation based on learners' needs. It elicits the information teachers need to learn more about their classroom and learners. The more that teachers encourage vulnerability and model it to students, the more that they will reduce the fear of making mistakes, which will allow them to gather robust student learning data. Through this cultural change and communication, teachers realize a more vulnerable classroom atmosphere focused on feedback and continual growth.

Interdependent Learning

Formative assessment and summative assessment are both important: "The formative and summative *purposes* of assessment must be interdependent to maximize learning and to verify achievement" (Erkens et al., 2017, p. 29). The heavy lifting of assessment must take place in the formative paradigm so that the summative assessment is truly a celebration and verification that learning has occurred.

Consider a competitive sport and the athlete's role and interactions at practices versus games. Coaches design practices around instruction and the needs of the athlete. Their role is to teach, intervene, and provide targeted feedback based on observations and assessments. They look for moments in which athletes might need redirection or additional practice and provide that intervention, whether it be with an individual, a small group, or the whole team. This is formative assessment and an instructional response *in action*. Coaches do the heavy lifting where it matters—in practices—so that they can be confident the athletes are ready for the game. Rarely, if ever, will a team choose not to engage in practices. The practices are a necessary part of learning because the athletes gain familiarity and confidence while receiving feedback and coaching to improve.

This idea parallels learning in the classroom. The heavy lifting must take place during the formative process (practices) so the teacher is confident that students are proficient when walking into the summative event (the game). Figure 1.1 (page 18) outlines a sample assessment plan that a teacher or teacher team could create in advance of a unit to confirm that students are ready for the summative assessment. An *x* indicates that the learning target is assessed. Tools such as figure 1.1 can be used at any grade level and with any discipline. With this unit, the teacher breaks down a standard into three learning targets and verifies that the summative assessment aligns to that standard. Through backward design, teachers ensure that they formatively assess each target at least three times to ensure readiness and allow for intervention throughout the learning. Keep in mind that in this model, formative assessment is displayed as a series of learning events (formal or informal) where data are collected in order to allow for an instructional response. (We address formative assessment in greater detail in chapters 4, page 73, and 5, page 91.)

	Formative Assessment 1	Formative Assessment 2	Formative Assessment 3	Formative Assessment 4	Formative Assessment 5	Formative Assessment 6	Formative Assessment 7	Summative Assessment
Learning Target 1	✓	✓		✓			✓	✓
Learning Target 2		✓	✓		✓		✓	✓
Learning Target 3				✓	✓	✓	✓	✓

FIGURE 1.1: Sample assessment plan.

Assessment in a Digital World

Defining assessment within the context of the ever-changing technological world does not deviate from the formative and summative purposes or the collaborative efforts that teachers and students engage in through the assessment process. No matter the instructional setting, in-person or remote learning, assessment is meant to be a window into students' thinking. It is essential that as teachers plan with standards for what proficiency looks like, they strive to design assessments and write assessment questions that assess students' true understanding of the standards, no matter the method of delivery. What teachers must carefully consider when assessing with technology is the way in which they seek evidence from students. Simple questions that students can answer with a quick internet search, or those that just ask students to regurgitate information, do not provide the evidence teachers need in order to plan future learning. Assessments should ask for original thinking or creativity in order to serve the purpose of assessment—to gather evidence of student learning in relation to the standards.

Learning for Teachers

Once teachers develop and understand their clear definitions and purposes for assessment, they are able to clarify the lens through which they view assessment and subsequent instruction. Assessment that teachers are using for formative purposes should answer the questions, Where are my students now? and What do they need to advance their proficiency? or even further, How can I use the data from this assessment to create learning plans that center on students and focus on growth? Assessment that teachers are using for summative purposes should answer the questions, How can I confirm that learning has occurred? and What product would I need to collect or what skills would I need to see demonstrated in order to confirm that students have reached proficiency? No matter whether students are early or late in the process of learning, repurposing and realigning assessment practices allows teachers to consider the question, What can I do to improve learning for each of my students?

While we address this topic with greater depth in chapter 3 (page 51), teachers should plan summative assessment so that the priority standards' intended rigor and the final destination are clear to the people responsible for formative instructional responses during learning. Teachers cannot answer the aforementioned questions with integrity if they lack a clear understanding of the needed final demonstration of learning. Because the purpose of summative assessment is the verification of learning, teachers will need to intermittently make adequate formative plans that ensure students are prepared for the summative event. Cassandra Erkens (2013), while talking about the balance between formative and summative assessment, states:

> The summatives should simply serve as a public celebration of how much learning has happened along the way. In this light, formative assessments might actually be the more "dull" because like the hard work of daily practice, they represent the little parts or scaffolding that can only lead to the big game.

With a common understanding of assessment purpose and use comes valuable learning for teachers. Through this lens, teachers should be designing an assessment process that will elicit the evidence necessary to answer the aforementioned questions. Teachers will no longer just evaluate student work; they will learn about what students know, how they learn best, what they do not know, and what needs to come next to coach them forward. For example, when creating an assessment that they intend to use formatively, teachers might focus on common misconceptions and develop an assessment that will give them the data to provide accurate in-class interventions the following day.

Learning for Students

When teachers define assessment and its purpose for students, they invite them to feel more comfortable with being active participants in the learning process. Meaningful assessment practices open up the communication between teachers and students and organically allow for more conversations centered on learning.

The key to using assessment formatively and ensuring student involvement and learning is what D. Royce Sadler (1989) refers to as the *feedback loop*. As the teacher provides feedback, the student then responds to that feedback, creating the loop. Imagine that a high school English language arts student hands in a writing assignment and the teacher responds in the following way:

> I really like the start you have with your analysis of the text. Remember that our focus is on using examples from the text to support your analysis. Can you please revisit that and distinguish what textual evidence you identified to support your analysis? Come show that to me when you are done. Great start, and I can't wait to see your next steps!

Notice that the teacher starts out with complimenting the student's work and then redirects him back to the targeted learning. The teacher then asks him to move his work forward by identifying textual support for his analysis and asks him to check in again. The teacher focuses not on what is missing or a grade but instead on next steps in order to improve the student's work. This changes the focus from *what was* to *what comes next.* In this situation, the student does not hear an evaluation or any negative remarks on his work; he hears the support of a teacher on what he needs to improve. This moment of assessment is learning for the student as he returns to his work to improve it.

Assessment should give students solid and empowering information on their strengths and point the way to their individualized next step to move forward. Formative assessment can significantly contribute to building student confidence and self-efficacy (Brookhart, 2013). When students succeed, their confidence rises. Thus, formative assessment should lead to what comes next instead of identifying what was wrong in student work; to assess is to move learning forward. When teachers keep the focus on growth, students tend to see misunderstandings and setbacks as a natural part of learning (Heritage, 2008; Shepard, 2000). This has the potential to change the overall classroom culture to one of vulnerability and learning, while allowing students to understand more about themselves as learners.

Through assessment, students must understand that they can and will learn, no matter where they start. Learners understand more about how they learn and how they can use the support of a teacher when they feel challenged or stuck. Following are some recommended guidelines to communicate about assessment with students and to guarantee students see assessment as a process of learning and growth.

- **Show that assessment is there to support learners:** Tell students that assessment is not always a moment to make a judgment but a moment to collect data to figure out how to better support them. Judgment will take place only after they receive ample time to practice and master the skill.

- **Highlight that assessment is a vulnerable process:** When asking students to engage in formative work, remind them that mistakes and questions are welcome and that errors help them grow.

- **Teach learners about the feedback loop:** Do not provide feedback unless there is a plan to have students act on it in order to create a culture of learning and feedback.

Defining and using assessment is truly a collaborative process. While this journey may start in a single classroom, it is essential to have a common and shared understanding within teacher teams. Many schools define themselves as PLCs, but all of these ideas can and should be used within any type of collaborative team.

Collaboration Around Assessment

In order to add a sense of structure and purpose to the assessment process as a whole, teachers and collaborative teams in schools and districts that function as PLCs use three big ideas and four critical questions to develop and evolve their understanding. The three big ideas of a PLC are (1) a focus on learning, (2) a collaborative culture and collective responsibility, and (3) a results orientation (DuFour et al., 2010, 2016). These ideas lie at the center of the assessment process. Defining and using assessment in its intended manner creates and supports a collaborative culture focused on learning and results. When teams come together to plan assessment, their response to results, and targeted intervention, collaboration fuels their learning as well as learning for students.

Using assessment as an instructional tool allows teachers to focus on learning over instruction. In that sense, teachers essentially do *less* day-to-day planning so they can implement *more* instructional agility based on emerging evidence of learning or a lack of learning. This focus on learning and the instructional response cannot happen unless teams first reach common understanding of the prioritized curricular standards, what proficiency looks like, and learning progressions (chapter 2, page 29).

With the complexity of curricular standards, taking on this assessment journey alone can be cumbersome and overwhelming. While it is achievable alone, creating a responsive and fluid assessment process benefits from a collaborative culture, which brings more voices to the table and makes everyone responsible for the learning. The assessment process starts with teacher teams coming together to provide accurate inferences and interpretations of the standards, reach agreed-on definitions and uses for formative and summative assessment, and achieve common understanding of the assessment process as a whole. An entire team of teachers possesses a wealth of knowledge when it comes to resources, content expertise, and instructional strategies. When teams pool their knowledge, they begin to take collective responsibility for all students, and everyone benefits. It is impossible to overemphasize the power of a teacher team when it comes to the question, What will we do when they haven't learned it?

Working to achieve a common understanding of assessment purpose and use is critical. If one teacher uses formative assessment to gather data, find errors and misconceptions, provide individualized feedback, and plan accordingly while another teacher simply scores formative assessment, it will lose its meaning, and these different uses will confuse students and parents. Effective collaboration ensures consistency so teachers can communicate that clarity to other stakeholders. Consider the following language that teachers could include in a syllabus, newsletter, or beginning-of-year communication with students and parents (figure 1.2).

Elementary School Example
In this classroom, the process of learning is never complete. This year, you will see your child bring home many papers with my feedback. Please take a moment to review that feedback, remind your child of the value of making mistakes and learning from them, and work together at home to improve. Grading will come when I feel that students are ready to show me their learning. Through the formative process, I want to focus on feedback and growth! Thanks for partnering with me on this journey!
Secondary Example
Assessment is a critical element of this classroom and will help me coach each learner forward. I will often collect or observe formative work and will return it with personalized narrative feedback. I will use this information to differentiate and monitor progress toward proficiency with our standards and learning targets. My promise to you is that the feedback I provide will be meaningful and will help you grow and improve! In order to be successful, learners will have to fully engage in the assessment process so that I can ensure all students are getting the coaching they need. I welcome mistakes, love questions, and can't wait for you to show me what you know!

FIGURE 1.2: Example communications to students and parents on the use of formative assessment.

Collaboration is critical to ensure that all teachers are on the same page with how they will use assessment and, equally important, how they will communicate its use and purpose to parents and students. It is not enough to take a definition and begin the assessment journey. All stakeholders should be invested in defining the terms and have a good understanding of how to use assessment and feedback to improve learning.

Teams are able to focus on student learning and results once their curriculum aligns to their priority standards, they agree on the intended rigor of those standards, they carefully design assessments, and they focus on instructional responses that are based on assessment evidence. With priority standards selected and learning progressions outlined, teams intentionally design checkpoints to collaborate and plan based on the needs of the classes and individuals. This personalizes the learning experience and brings more ideas to the intervention stages of responsive instruction. Team-developed common assessments ensure that teachers come to collaborate with a focus on next steps and results.

These three big ideas help teams ground themselves. The four critical questions help them organize their work. The four critical questions of a PLC are as follows (DuFour et al., 2010, 2016), along with how they align with the assessment process.

1. What do students need to know and be able to do? (priority standards)

2. How will we know when they have learned it? (individual- and team-developed assessments)

3. What will we do when they haven't learned it? (systematic intervention)

4. What will we do when they already know it? (enrichment)

Assessment not only guides teaching and learning but also sheds light on where intervention or enrichment might be necessary, which students need it, and to what extent they need it.

When teams ask what students need to know and be able to do, they are providing themselves a means of clearly understanding what their common destination is. If they do not have a clear goal (the standard) in place, the team cannot effectively use the process of sound assessment to design learning experiences, provide feedback, and move learners closer to that desired outcome. In order to start planning any units of study or developing learning progressions (as outlined in chapter 2, page 29), teams will need to determine their priority standards and intended outcomes, including rigor level, for the learning sequence. Having this goal in place also makes collaborative discussions as a team productive and worthwhile. This goal sets the stage for meaningful learning for both teachers and students.

When teams consider how they will know when students have learned it, it is helpful to think about two questions, How can I confirm that learning has occurred? and What product would I need to collect or what skills would I need to see demonstrated in order to confirm that students have reached proficiency? before the beginning of a new unit of study. This normally comes in the form of team-designed assessments with common rubrics outlining what proficiency should look or sound like. This may also include student exemplars of proficiency. A student's grade should not depend on the classroom or teacher; there should be a common understanding of proficiency among teacher teams. This common understanding will ground the assessment process so that teachers make all instructional decisions with that end goal in mind.

Using assessments formatively lends itself to determining what to do when students have not learned it. While a one-size-fits-all instruction and assessment classroom might be ideal, it is not realistic, and formative assessment provides the information necessary to meet the needs of individuals while keeping the common destination in mind. Involving all members of a collaborative team will lead the team to gather more ideas and resources into its tool kit of instructional responses and interventions. This collaborative work will allow team members to look at common misconceptions and needs and brainstorm targeted instructional responses based on those needs. When using a tool such as figure 1.3 (page 26), teachers develop the expertise to recognize struggles and pull from a host of actions designed to target misconceptions.

It is also important for teams to keep in mind what to do when students already know it. All students in the classroom deserve a full year's worth of learning, even if they come in already able to demonstrate some of the intended outcomes. As teams discuss the process of assessment, it is essential that they outline how enrichment can occur and what that learning will look or sound like. While working collaboratively through the use of assessment, team members should consider the following questions.

- How will we know if students are proficient with the intended learning?

- How will we respond when a student displays proficiency early? What will enrichment look like?

Most importantly, teacher teams must again collaboratively brainstorm the next steps for those learners (see figure 1.3) and consider how differentiation should help enrich and encourage continual growth.

Standard: Determine whether a group of objects (up to 20) has an odd or even number of members, e.g., by pairing objects or counting them by 2s; write an equation to express an even number as a sum of two equal addends. (2.OA.C.3)

Misconception 1: Addition errors	Misconception 2: Understanding even versus odd	Students who are approaching proficiency:	Students who need enrichment:
Students with this misconception:	Students with this misconception:		
Plan: Use manipulatives to have students model addition.	Plan: Work with ten frame to have students model numbers.	Plan: Students continue to practice the targeted skill.	Plan: Students develop equations with even or odd sums.

Source for standard: National Governors Association Center for Best Practices (NGA) & Council of Chief State School Officers (CCSSO), 2010b.

FIGURE 1.3: Collaborative brainstorming template.

*Visit **go.SolutionTree.com/assessment** for a free reproducible version of this figure.*

QUESTIONS for
Reflection

*Use these questions to reflect on this chapter's
learning and begin to look forward.*

1. How does our team or school define and understand formative
    assessment and summative assessment? Do we need to revisit
    these definitions and understandings?

2. How do we communicate our assessment purposes to students
    and families?

3. Reflecting on the assessment truths (page 9), what is an area of
    assessment that we need to improve on? How will improving
    this strengthen learning for our students?

4. What are some simple language changes that we can implement
    in our classrooms and school to create a culture centered
    on learning?

5. Do students in our school view assessment as a process and tool
    that supports their learning? Why or why not?

Next Steps for Defining Assessment

Define assessment as a team.

Understand how assessment will be used
(both formatively and summatively).

Communicate that definition, and use
it with both students and parents.

Design assessment experiences that allow
for feedback and an instructional response.

Remind students to be vulnerable in the
assessment process, and use the feedback
loop to keep students involved.

Frequently reassess and look for ways to
increase communication and learning.

chapter two

LEARNING PROGRESSIONS

*The first step towards getting
somewhere is to decide you're not
going to stay where you are.*

—John Pierpont Morgan

Throughout learning, step-by-step guidance allows students and teachers to see progress and accomplishment along the way. Learning progressions chart this progress and clarify curricular standards that are often complex and include multiple skills. These progressions supply teachers with an instructional guide and give students manageable steps that lead to achievement. They foster student-teacher relationships by creating a common set of goals and benchmarks that students and teachers work toward together. Teachers can target and center feedback and next steps on the shared destination. A learning progression ensures that all stakeholders are invested in the journey, supporting learning and striving for consistency across teams, schools, and districts. After setting a learning progression, teachers and teams can intentionally plan assessment to ensure they are using it to its full capacity.

What Is It?

For the purpose of this book, we define a *learning progression* as a series of learning targets (broken-down pieces of a priority standard) that teachers sequence from simplest to most complex. Learning progressions are the foundational elements for assessment design and decisions and provide a clear road map for both students and teachers. They derive from the standards that teachers have prioritized for each content area, grade level, or course. Essentially, they are intentional sequences of learning targets to guide learning, practice, and the path to proficiency. According to W. James Popham (2007), "Identifying 'must-learn' building blocks enables teachers to plan instructional sequences that give students systematic rather than sporadic opportunities to master each building block in the learning progression" (p. 83).

Learning progressions tie the end goal (standards) to daily experiences and interactions in the classroom. Imagine a sixth-grade student is going to be working with a new standard such as this one: "Trace and evaluate the argument and specific claims in a text, distinguishing claims that are supported by reasons and evidence from claims that are not" (RI.6.8; NGA & CCSSO, 2010a). Not only does this standard include multiple verbs (*trace*, *evaluate*, and *distinguish*), but it also has a good amount of context for those skills (*argument*, *specific claims*, *reasons*, and *evidence*) that could be very difficult for sixth-grade students to comprehend. When teachers create and effectively use learning progressions in the classroom, there is seamless communication between what students are learning and what comes next. When teachers then gauge proficiency throughout a unit of study, learning progressions are tightly connected to daily instruction and practice as a natural part of learning. Checking in on each target of a learning progression strongly bonds assessment to learning.

What we refer to as *learning progressions* in this book can take on many other names in the education realm, such as *learning targets*, *learning goals*, *learning ladders*, *benchmarks*, *"I can" statements*, and the like. Their name does not matter as much as their alignment to the standards and their usefulness in the classroom. We use the term *learning progression* in this book because it indicates there is a sequence to the content and underpinning skills (targets) that students develop over time. It is this sequencing from simplest to most complex that brings learning together to communicate a journey, as opposed to a simple list.

It is important to state that learning progressions are not rubrics. Rubrics refer to the quality of students' work once they have demonstrated the larger skill that the standard describes. Learning progressions comprise scaled steps (smaller skills) in the process of learning to achieve proficiency with the standard (larger skill). Once they have mastered the steps, students are ready to put the standard together again and demonstrate their proficiency. It is at this point that a teacher would use a rubric—once the students can perform the skill or skills stated in the standard, not the smaller skills within the learning progression.

The following sections outline how to design learning progressions, and then move into using them.

Priority Standards and the Design of Learning Progressions

The assessment process begins by (1) identifying priority standards, and (2) building learning progressions for those priority standards by creating and ordering the learning targets from simplest to most complex. The following sections break down these steps for teachers or teacher teams.

Prioritizing Standards

Teachers should not break down all standards for a particular content area or course into learning progressions. Usually, the standards for each subject in a grade level are quite copious. For example, the Common Core State Standards for eighth-grade mathematics total twenty-eight robust standards (NGA & CCSSO, 2010b). This does not include the numerous sub-standards that many of those standards include or the eight Mathematical Practices that round out this Common Core resource. Creating step-by-step learning progressions for all those standards would be a huge task, and it is not necessary. Prioritizing standards before creating learning progressions makes this process more manageable.

In determining the standards that they should deem priorities for a course or grade level, teachers have four characteristics to consider: (1) endurance, (2) leverage, (3) readiness, and (4) external exam requirements (Ainsworth, 2013). Here are helpful questions to consider alongside those four characteristics to guide discussions on the prioritization of standards.

1. **Endurance:** Does the standard endure throughout the school year or from year to year?

2. **Leverage:** Does the standard include a skill or skills that cross over into other content areas?

3. **Readiness:** Does the standard include an essential skill or skills that students will need for the next grade level or course?

4. **External exam requirements:** Are there particular standards that are of high need for our learning community?

Standards do not have to fit all four descriptors in order to be prioritized; these are simply ideas that can frame those prioritization decisions.

Building Learning Progressions

After selecting priority standards, teachers can move to deconstructing those standards. In order to create a learning progression, teachers must deconstruct, or unpack, the priority standard or standards within a unit. In her book *The Handbook for Collaborative Common Assessments*, Cassandra Erkens (2019) provides a thorough protocol for deconstructing standards as well as unpacking them into learning targets. Those targets form a learning progression when sequenced from simplest to most complex. Figure 2.1 (page 32) outlines eight of the nine steps Erkens (2019) identifies and explains. The ninth step of the protocol is omitted here because it includes a detailed plan for assessment. Planning for summative and formative assessment using both the standards and learning progressions (step 9) will be discussed

Step 1	Read the entire standard, and come to agreement on what it means when everything is put together. What evidence would students have to produce and at what level of rigor would the assessment tasks need to be in order to meet the entirety of the standard?
Step 2	Highlight (or circle if on paper) all the verbs. What will students need to do to complete this standard?
Step 3	Underline any part of the standard that will require direct instruction in order for students to be successful.
Step 4	Bold (or star if on paper) any skills that require direct observation. You will specifically watch or listen for these items with each student during a performance task. *Note: You may find standards that do not fit this criterion.*
Step 5	Italicize (or box if on paper) any items or quality indicators that need to be part of the required products for standard completion. *Note: Many standards do not delineate the specific products that students must develop.*
Step 6	Identify the context and the content that you will use to teach and assess the standard.
Step 7	Create a student-friendly progression of learning targets for the content and process standard. *Note: It is helpful to list and rank the targets from simplest to most complex.*
Step 8	Develop a brief description of a summative assessment needed to measure student learning on the standard or standards selected.

Source: Adapted from Erkens, 2019.

FIGURE 2.1: Protocol for unpacking standards.

further in chapters 3–5 (pages 51–114). Not every standard will require all the steps; those steps that may not apply to all standards are indicated in the figure.

This protocol not only provides steps for creating learning progressions but also initiates thinking and collaborative conversation about formative and summative assessment. It provides the starting place for planning a unit with backward design—beginning with what students should know, understand, and be able to do followed by how teachers will assess those skills. The interaction among standards, learning progressions, and assessment produces an environment centered on learning.

When developing learning progressions, as seen in figure 2.2, it is plain to see that alignment is critical. Beyond addressing the pieces of the standards in full, learning progressions should feature targets that address prerequisite skills as well as enrichment; these targets are valuable for students and teachers to maintain focus on continual learning. Imagine that students are starting at ground level and climbing a ladder—what is their simple, yet slightly more complex, next step to progress closer to the intended goal? Knowing that they possess necessary prerequisite skills and seeing themselves on a progression from the beginning can build learners' confidence. Targets that address enrichment communicate to students that learning never stops, and even if they achieve proficiency, there is a way to keep progressing.

Using the protocol in figure 2.1, figure 2.2 breaks down the aforementioned sixth-grade English language arts standard (RI.6.8; NGA & CCSSO, 2010a) into a learning progression.

Step 1: Read the entire standard, and come to agreement on what it means when everything is put together. What evidence would students have to produce and at what level of rigor would the assessment tasks need to be in order to meet the entirety of the standard?	Trace and evaluate the argument and specific claims in a text, distinguishing claims that are supported by reasons and evidence from claims that are not. (RI.6.8)
Step 2: Highlight (or circle if on paper) all the verbs. What will students need to do to complete this standard?	Trace and evaluate the argument and specific claims in a text, distinguishing claims that are supported by reasons and evidence from claims that are not.
Step 3: Underline any part of the standard that will require direct instruction in order for students to be successful.	Trace and evaluate the argument and specific claims in a text, distinguishing claims that are supported by reasons and evidence from claims that are not.
Step 4: Bold (or star if on paper) any skills that require direct observation. You will specifically watch or listen for these items with each student during a performance task. Note: You may find standards that do not fit this criterion.	Trace and evaluate the argument and specific claims in a text, distinguishing claims that are supported by reasons and evidence from claims that are not. (This standard does not have any skills that must be directly observed.)

FIGURE 2.2: Example standard broken down into learning targets with the unpacking protocol.   continued ▶

Step 5: Italicize (or box if on paper) any items or quality indicators that need to be part of the required products for standard completion. *Note: Many standards do not delineate the specific products that students must develop.*	Trace and evaluate the argument and specific claims in a text, distinguishing claims that are supported by reasons and evidence from claims that are not. *(This standard does not have a delineated product.)*
Step 6: Identify the context and the content that you will use to teach and assess the standard.	**Context:** This standard will be presented in a social studies unit on current events. This will be the second time this school year that this skill is practiced and demonstrated. **Content:** Since the standard asks students to work with an argument and claims, the content of their text will need to be argumentative.
Step 7: Create a student-friendly progression of learning targets for the content and process standard. *Note: It is helpful to list and rank the targets from simplest to most complex.*	• Identify the author's point of view or purpose in a text (simplest). • Explain how an author uses evidence to support particular points in a text. • Define *argument* and *claim*. • Identify the argument and claim the author presents in a text. • Distinguish claims that are supported by facts from claims that are supported by opinions. • Evaluate the argument and claims using evidence from the text. • Determine whether claims in a text are or are not supported by reasons or evidence (most complex).
Step 8: Develop a brief description of a summative assessment needed to measure student learning on the standards selected.	As part of a writing assignment, students will have to show mastery of this standard. They will be writing an argumentative essay that will include multiple valid and reliable sources that support their claims.

Source: Adapted from Erkens, 2019.
Source for standard: NGA & CCSSO, 2010a.

Visit **go.SolutionTree.com/assessment** *for a free reproducible version of this figure.*

Since the example in figure 2.2 does not have any skills that teachers must observe and it does not lay out a specific product that must result, figure 2.3 identifies examples of standards that would fit those criteria and in turn be bolded or italicized in the unpacking process.

Observable Skills
Demonstrate safe procedures for using and cleaning art tools, equipment, and studio spaces. (VA:Cr2.2.2a)
I can express some basic needs, using practiced or memorized words and phrases in Spanish. (Adapted from Interpersonal Communication Novice.2.NL)
Required Products
Develop models to describe that organisms have unique and diverse life cycles but all have in common birth, growth, reproduction, and death. (3-LS1-1)
Write arguments to support claims in an analysis of substantive topics or texts, using valid reasoning and relevant and sufficient evidence. (W.9-10.1)

Source for standards: American Council on the Teaching of Foreign Languages, 2017; National Coalition for Core Arts Standards, 2014; NGA & CCSSO, 2010a; NGSS Lead States, 2013.

FIGURE 2.3: Examples of standards that include observable skills and require products.

The non-negotiable element of building learning progressions is that they must align to the standard and communicate the path to proficiency.

Organizing Learning Progressions

Since teachers construct learning progressions in sequence of complexity, students may find it helpful to gain some distinction among the prerequisite targets, the proficiency targets, and the enrichment targets. In her book *Softening the Edges*, Katie White (2017) provides four stages for creating a learning continuum: (1) building readiness, (2) exploring the learning goal, (3) clarifying proficiency, and (4) enriching understanding. We've adapted this useful framework to offer four levels that teachers can use to categorize targets within a progression to show how they are used in the classroom setting. This organization can be used no matter the length of the list of learning targets.

1. **Readiness-building targets:** These targets address the prerequisite skills, such as prior knowledge and vocabulary, that students should

possess as they enter learning with the standard. The purpose of readiness-building targets is preassessment or early formative assessment to provide intervention and ensure readiness to engage with the new content and skills.

2. **Exploration targets:** These targets address the daily instruction and scaffolding at a lower Depth of Knowledge level than the standard requires (Webb, 2002). The purpose of these targets in the formative realm is to lay a solid foundation and provide intervention during early learning.

3. **Proficiency targets:** These targets outline the steps needed to develop proficiency with the standard. It is important to note that for summative purposes, the standard is what is assessed. The targets are the underpinnings necessary to show proficiency with the larger skill. These targets are for formative use in the classroom (to provide feedback and ongoing intervention) and guide summative assessment (to put the targets back together to confirm that learning has occurred).

4. **Targets for enriched understanding:** These targets address a deeper understanding and skill level of the standard. These are written to address the question, What if students have already learned it? and offer teachers a shared understanding of how to allow for differentiation and challenge once learners are proficient. While the goal is proficiency with the standard, teachers write these targets so they can push students beyond proficiency.

Figure 2.4 is an example of a fifth-grade science learning progression that uses the four levels to categorize its targets. In order for students to show proficiency, they would have to demonstrate mastery at level 3 (proficiency). The additional targets at level 4 (enriched understanding) are for students who are ready for enrichment and extension.

In addition to the creation and organization of learning progressions, teachers and teacher teams must be mindful of using a manageable number of targets and student-friendly language.

Standard: Investigate and share the characteristics and physical properties of material in solid, liquid, and gaseous states of matter.		
More Complex	Enriched Understanding	• I can design experiments that test unique questions. • I can explain how solids, liquids, and gases are complex and sometimes difficult to categorize. • I can propose strategies for determining states of matter for unknown substances.
	Proficiency	• I can create an investigation that includes experimenting, classifying, asking questions, and measuring. • I can clearly share physical properties using accurate descriptors. • I can clearly share physical properties as they relate to all states of matter.
Less Complex	Exploration	• I can describe the components of a good investigation. • I can ask questions related to my experiment. • I can measure accurately. • I can classify information as it relates to my experiment. • I can describe the difference between a solid, liquid, and gas.
	Readiness Building	• I can explain a physical property. • I can define *characteristic*. • I can explain how states of matter can be different and give an example. • I can use descriptive language.

Source: Adapted from Dimich, 2015; White, 2017.
Source for standard: Unpublished adapted standard, K. White, personal communication, March, 2021.

FIGURE 2.4: Sample learning progression with targets categorized by level of proficiency.

A Manageable Number of Targets

A recurring question arises through this process: How many learning targets are appropriate in a learning progression? As the previous examples have demonstrated, the number of targets will vary depending on the standard, teacher (or teacher team), and students. There is no definitive answer as to how many but plenty of guidance to help with making this decision.

Learning progressions must be manageable for students and teachers. If there are too many targets, students may feel that the journey to achievement with the standard is very long and potentially inaccessible. The end goal can be lost in the process. Another concern that arises with a long list of learning targets is the targets can become individual activities for the classroom rather than skills students are developing in a variety of ways.

On the other end of the spectrum, if a learning progression has few targets but those steps are too complex, it can again seem unmanageable for students in the short term. When considering the number of learning targets to include in a progression, teachers must keep in mind the importance of targets that directly address the standard as well as those that provide additional scaffolding for all learners. To help determine how many targets are appropriate, ask yourself, "Can students place themselves on this ladder, see their growth, and envision next steps?"

Learning Progression Language

"The development of learning progressions is about intentionally sequencing instruction from the simplest (targets) to the most sophisticated (standards) demonstrations of learning" (Schimmer, Hillman, & Stalets, 2018, p. 34). Teachers must consider the language they use for these progressions; each one must balance academic language with language that ensures that students are able to comprehend and use it. If the progressions are inaccessible for students because of the complexity of language, they lose their value and become something that teachers have only *created* rather than something they have *created and use* as an ongoing process.

When deciding whether a verb in a learning target is specific enough, Nicole Dimich (2015) asks an important question, which she includes in her book *Design in Five*: "What would the student work look like that would represent a student's achievement of this standard, or learning goal?" (p. 28). If the student work would serve as a building block for eventually demonstrating achievement of the standard, the target is appropriate. Figure 2.5 provides sample learning targets pulled from a progression. This is not a complete learning progression; just two of the targets appear with examples of how teachers could make them either too specific or too complex. Ensuring that targets are specific skills for the students to work with without being reduced to classroom activities is essential.

Standard: Analyze, select, and curate artifacts and/or artworks for presentation and preservation. (VA:Pr4.1.Ia)			
	Too Specific	**Appropriate**	**Too Complex**
Learning Target 1	Choose five criteria for selecting artifacts and artwork that will be presented or preserved.	Determine criteria for selecting artifacts and artwork that will be presented or preserved.	Explore the criteria for quality artifacts and artwork.
Learning Target 2	Using a database of artwork, choose three pieces to analyze using our design protocol.	Analyze artwork using the established criteria.	Analyze a piece of artwork.

Source for standard: National Coalition for Core Arts Standards, 2014.

FIGURE 2.5: Sample learning targets.

Considerations such as the age of the learners and the Depth of Knowledge level of the standard (Webb, 2002) shed additional light on how detailed a learning progression might be. Teachers demonstrate the power of learning progressions when they use them to guide daily classroom activities and interactions. In time, students will follow the model of their teacher and internalize the process as well.

The Use of Learning Progressions

Learning progressions provide for tight alignment with the learning that will build proficiency toward the standards. (And learning progressions serve as a daily guide for formative assessment, the process of which chapters 4, page 73, and 5, page 91, will delve deeply into.) Teachers must make learning progressions visible to students, whether they post the progressions in the classroom, use them for preassessment at the outset of new learning, or include learning targets from them at the top of an assignment. Beyond seeing the learning progression, the students and teacher must interact with the targets in order for them to be useful. It is best that teachers consistently remind students of the skills they are working on as well as how the skills contribute to achievement with the standard as a whole. There are times when teachers find it effective to provide students the entire progression of targets at the beginning of a unit of study to plainly communicate the journey students are to embark on. If this is likely to overwhelm students, teachers can chunk the targets into smaller groups and communicate each group as learning increases in complexity. If students begin disengaging from the learning process because they feel like they will never achieve the standard, it is time to go back to the learning progression and let them see the small steps that will help them toward the goal.

Progressions should not feel like an extra activity in the classroom unless teachers are developing them with students. In that case, the previously mentioned protocol for deconstructing and unpacking standards in figure 2.1 (page 32) is useful. Whether progressions are teacher or student created, once in place, they should play a seamless role in daily happenings. The learning progression naturally flows with the activities students engage with and makes the purpose of each activity plain. Progressions can also take a more formal role, such as with the teacher opening class with a very specific focus on the target or targets for the day. Again, this goes beyond displaying a target on the board; the progression frames learning and grounds instruction and practice for students. The more that teachers use learning progressions in a meaningful way in the classroom, the easier it will be for students to achieve them. This ensures there is no confusion as to what knowledge, understandings, and skills students are developing and what evidence will prove proficiency.

With the learning progression in place, teachers can begin to consider how the assessment process will work and make sure that students are invested.

Building an Assessment Process

In *Essential Assessment*, authors Cassandra Erkens, Tom Schimmer, and Nicole Dimich (2017) explain the importance of viewing assessment as ongoing—that is, as the process of assessing, a verb. It is a fluid process that includes and links both formative and summative assessment. Within the formative realm, learning progressions play a pivotal role in the movement of student learning. When assessment tools and processes align to learning targets, student evidence of proficiency with the targets is explicit. The progression clearly guides instruction and student practice. From there, teachers can employ the architecture of assessment and form and implement new tools. In *Essential Assessment*, Erkens and her colleagues (2017) use the analogy of a house when discussing assessment architecture—the standards and criteria for quality are the specifications; the assessment designs (including formative and summative assessments) are the architectural blueprint; the curriculum and content are the concrete, forms, and walls; and finally, the instruction is the paint and decor that make each house unique.

Learning progressions should build confidence for learners as they progress, and the most complex targets should begin to mirror what the learners will have to do to demonstrate proficiency with summative assessment. Although teachers are not using the smaller skills from progressions to create summative assessment items per se, these smaller skills do play an important role in ensuring students are ready to begin the summative process.

The idea that assessment should be planned in advance of instruction lends itself perfectly to learning progressions. However, it is important to note that teachers will also have assessment opportunities that are not necessarily determined prior to a unit of study, such as the moments when they work with students one-on-one during class (addressed in chapter 4, page 73). Just as the learning targets grow in complexity as they approach the level of the standard, so must the planning of assessment, instruction, and practice. The interworking of all these parts creates clear opportunities to gauge student proficiency on the part of both the teacher and the student and make informed decisions that will ultimately deliver achievement with the standards.

Ensuring Student Investment

Student investment with learning progressions enhances the progressions' relevance and usefulness in the classroom. If students do not engage with the progression, it is at best a tool only the teacher uses and at worst something that the teacher might post in the room and forget about. To invest in their learning, students should spend time getting familiar with the sequence of targets, which in turn helps them better understand the larger standard and how they will learn. They should understand what the skill looks or sounds like in action. When students and teachers create a shared understanding of the end goal and the steps required to get there, they strengthen the connection between the progression and the standard. A learning progression is a series of collective goals designed for students and educators to achieve together.

Students invest when they are an integral part of the process. As mentioned, teachers can develop learning progressions together with the students. When the class develops targets together, teachers play a very important role. They must initiate the conversation with students about the standards and their meaning. It is also helpful to have examples of student work on hand to show the learners what the end product or learning will look or sound like. From there, the class can begin to discuss how to break down the standards. It is important to remember there will be skills that must be part of the progression that students may not identify. Students do not know what they do not know, so some building blocks will be harder to pinpoint than others for the learners. Moving forward, students and teachers can come together to make decisions about learning, feedback, and next steps.

Learning for Teachers

Breaking down standards into targets and putting the targets in a natural progression from simplest to most complex is an effective way for teachers themselves to truly expand their understanding of the standards. They must consider what the standards demand of the student in the end and what evidence will be accepted as proficient. Once teachers develop this understanding, they can create learning progressions with concrete steps that students will use to understand their own progress and that teachers will use for planning and assessment.

Teachers can also use learning progressions to preplan enrichment and intervention. Teachers can ready themselves ahead of time by anticipating mistakes and errors and gathering resources for early intervention and response within the classroom setting. At the same time, inevitably, some students will achieve at high levels throughout the progression; teachers can also plan enrichment for them.

Teachers can easily use the learning progression with students as a checklist of understanding (acknowledging that the complexity increases throughout the progression), personalizing students' place in the progression and allowing for differentiated experiences based on immediate needs. This supports teachers as they learn about and form relationships with students. Teachers can glean a good amount of information simply from assessment evidence; however, no assessment can tell the entire story of the student. By using learning progressions to facilitate a conversation, teachers reinforce the skills that students are building and either affirm their thinking or gain insight about assumptions that turned out to be incorrect.

For example, imagine a fourth-grade student is working with the learning target, "Determine the main idea of a story," and so far, the teacher feels she is making adequate progress with the skill. The teacher has delivered instruction on how to find the main idea and how to decide whether something is a main idea or key detail. The class has practiced as a whole and in small groups, and this student has volunteered good, well-thought-out answers. Since she volunteers correct answers in a group setting, the teacher may feel that the student is ready for the next target in the progression, which is "Use key details to explain the main idea of a story." However, through individual assessment and talking with the student, the teacher determines that the student has not yet had enough practice to consistently demonstrate the first target. She may be able to work with peers to find the main idea but is struggling to do it on her own. At this moment, the teacher is not only learning more about the student's proficiency level but also continuing to form a strong relationship with the student by taking the time to individually address her needs.

Learning for Students

Students benefit from and need an in-depth understanding of the standards teachers expect them to learn and master throughout a unit of study or school year. For students to obtain this understanding, learning targets and a sense of how they build on one another are essential. Not only do students gain knowledge about their final destination, but they also begin to see the way forward to achieve that goal. Learners need to know where they are going, and they need confidence that the end goal is attainable. According to John Hattie (as cited in Visible Learning, n.d.), teacher clarity has an effect size (the measure he uses for the impact of education initiatives) of 0.76, meaning it has a significant positive effect on student learning. The impact of clarity on student learning has the potential to accelerate learning (Visible Learning, n.d.). This clarity derives from the deep understanding of priority standards, the deconstruction of those standards, and the creation of learning progressions. These progressions also support a growth mindset, where students can continually look forward in their learning and develop self-efficacy (Dweck, 2016).

Students will learn more about themselves as learners when they utilize progressions. They can see how they learn best and gauge their pacing. Consider this scenario: Second-grade students are working through a unit of study in social studies. The teacher hands out the learning progression and the reflection tool (figure 2.6) at the beginning of the unit and instructs students to keep them in their social studies folders. With support and modeling, the teacher invites the students to reflect on their experience and understanding after a classroom activity. Figure 2.6 is an example of a reflection tool that lists learning targets and provides room for students to write in classroom activities and record when they mastered those particular targets.

Standard: Explain how weather, climate, and other environmental characteristics affect people's lives in a place or region. (D2.Geo.4.K-2)		
Learning Targets	Activities and Practice	Date Mastered
Define *weather, climate,* and *environmental characteristics*.		
Describe weather, climate, and environmental characteristics for a particular region.		

FIGURE 2.6: Learning target self-assessment template 1.   continued ▶

Explain how weather impacts people from a particular region.		
Explain how climate impacts people from a particular region.		
Explain how environmental characteristics impact people from a particular region.		

Source for standard: National Council for the Social Studies, 2017.

*Visit **go.SolutionTree.com/assessment** for a free reproducible version of this figure.*

A tool such as this can be used to let students know the steps in their learning and to help them reflect on that learning over time. Elementary students will need help when starting this process but will become more independent once they have practice. Secondary students may understand how to work through the process but may need support in following through with it. Reflecting in this way can help students articulate how things are working for them and their learning so they can self-advocate.

Another way teachers can facilitate learning through student self-assessment with targets is shown in figure 2.7, which lists a first-grade physical education standard and learning target and allows students space to indicate their proficiency level a few different times as they practice and progress. While the previous example allows students to list activities that are aligned to each target and indicate when they mastered that particular target, this tool allows students to self-assess in an ongoing manner to see growth as they progress through learning. By the end of the unit, both teachers and students should have confidence that the students will demonstrate proficiency on the summative assessment.

By involving students in the development and use of learning targets, teachers encourage them to invest in their learning. Students can see their progress, and that success motivates them. Learning is a matter of *when* rather than *if*. This focus on student learning when using learning progressions is also critical to how teachers and

Standard: The physically literate individual demonstrates competency in a variety of motor skills and movement patterns. (Standard 1)		
Learning Target	**Date and Activity**	**Mastery Level** (Circle one.)
I can demonstrate locomotor skills (running, hopping, jumping, skipping, and so on) in a variety of activities.		I'm just getting started I'm on my way I've got this!
		I'm just getting started I'm on my way I've got this!
		I'm just getting started I'm on my way I've got this!
		I'm just getting started I'm on my way I've got this!

Source for standard: SHAPE America—Society of Health and Physical Educators, 2013.

FIGURE 2.7: Learning target self-assessment template 2.

*Visit **go.SolutionTree.com/assessment** for a free reproducible version of this figure.*

teams collaborate. If teachers have developed learning progressions in the classroom alongside students, then it is imperative that they bring those progressions to collaborative team meetings to share and find common ground.

Collaboration Around Assessment

When teachers work in collaborative teams, developing and discussing learning progressions is essential. Individual understanding of the standards and learning progressions is powerful and very important; collective understanding is even more important. Collaborative teams must meet to discuss priority standards and learning progressions before embarking on the journey of assessment. Without this prerequisite, there is no consistency in the learning that they expect of students.

When teachers work together to identify essential learning through standards and progressions, they have a clear focus on learning and results while working collaboratively—encompassing all three of the big ideas of a PLC (DuFour et al., 2016). Teams maintain a focus on learning by discussing and making decisions about what students will need to know, understand, and be able to do. They continually build a collaborative culture through these meetings and discussions as long as there are clear norms for the meetings that all team members honor and follow (DuFour et al., 2016). These norms are essential to ensure the team hears and considers all voices along the way, the teachers use the meeting time productively, and the team is action oriented. The results orientation comes through the assessment process, and learning progressions play a vital role in determining what supports must be in place to ensure the desired student achievement result.

Although teams need to consider all four questions when prioritizing standards and developing learning progressions, the one they must focus on the most from the beginning is question 1 (What do students need to know and be able to do? DuFour et al., 2016). We will expand on how questions 2, 3, and 4 impact learning progressions in later chapters.

When a collaborative team sets out on the task of developing these progressions, consensus about priority standards must take place first. While most content areas have very long lists of standards provided at the state, provincial, or national levels, there is no need to feel overwhelmed. Rather, using the aforementioned parameters (page 31) to choose priority standards ensures that the curriculum is, as assessment expert and researcher Robert J. Marzano (2017) puts it, guaranteed and viable. A guaranteed curriculum is one that has consistency with the essential learning each student will have access to no matter which teacher is leading the classroom. Teachers achieve viability when they can accomplish that curriculum in a meaningful manner within the confines of a given school year (Marzano, 2017). Teams must consider viability when determining the quantity of priority standards in order for the curriculum to be guaranteed. Again, only the prioritized standards require the development of learning progressions.

Analyzing standards and creating learning progressions has profound outcomes for all members of the PLC. In *Learning by Doing*, authors Richard DuFour, Rebecca DuFour, Robert Eaker, Thomas W. Many, and Mike Mattos (2016) provide five reasons why determining essential learning in a PLC promotes a guaranteed and viable curriculum. Essential learning encompasses the prioritized standards as well as the learning progressions derived from them:

Collaborative study of essential learning—

1. Promotes clarity

2. Promotes consistent priorities

3. Is crucial to the common pacing required for formative assessments

4. Can help establish a curriculum that is viable

5. Creates ownership of the curriculum among those who are asked to teach it (DuFour et al., 2016, p. 125)

The collaborative learning gained through team discussions and decisions about standards and learning progressions launches effective assessment processes. These five reasons guide not only the determination of essential learning; teachers and teams can also use them to navigate summative and formative assessment. Clarity, alignment, pacing, and ownership all play key roles moving forward.

Questions for
Reflection

*Use these questions to reflect on this chapter's
learning and begin to look forward.*

1. Does our team have a common method for unpacking standards into learning targets?

2. Are our learning targets carefully crafted with student-friendly language?

3. Do our learning targets follow a natural sequence from simplest to most complex to form a learning progression?

4. Does the team have a common understanding of what high-quality student work would look or sound like with each step of the learning progression?

5. Does the learning progression guide team decisions about assessment, instruction, and practice?

Next Steps for Prioritizing Standards and Developing Learning Progressions

Collaboratively prioritize standards in your team or professional learning community.

For each prioritized standard, discuss what proficiency would look or sound like for the standard.

Deconstruct the prioritized standards, and create learning progressions based on the steps needed to demonstrate mastery.

Using the prioritized standards and learning progressions, plan for formative and summative assessment (addressed in chapters 3 [page 51], 4 [page 73], and 5 [page 91]).

Use the learning progressions with students for instruction and practice.

Use the learning progressions for student reflection and self-assessment.

chapter three

SUMMATIVE ASSESSMENT

*Never stop learning; for when we
stop learning, we stop growing.*

—Loyal "Jack" Lewman

Summative assessment can seem like it is the end of learning, but each stage of assessment, including summative, serves a purpose in expanding students' knowledge, their thinking, and how to proceed. When teachers plan summative assessment prior to beginning a unit of study, they can be more intentional with feedback, assessment, and instructional practices, as they have clearly determined the intended learning outcomes and their level of rigor. The goal of summative assessment is to confirm what teachers already know about student proficiency, but it is not always foolproof. There are times when students do not meet anticipated proficiency levels; these are opportunities for everyone in the classroom to learn more about what comes next.

This chapter addresses the sometimes overlooked learning that arises from the summative assessment process. This process provides for a moment of reflection for both teachers and students. Students receive a chance to give their teachers feedback and reflect on their own proficiency, and teachers learn more about what students' preferences are and how an assessment method did or did not accurately gauge their proficiency. Both gain valuable information regarding mistakes and errors, which teachers can use to determine whether there is a lack of proficiency or a lack of clarity within the assessment tool that they must address. Summative assessment is simply a pause that provides an opportunity to gather robust information and evidence of learning at that moment in time (Garrison & Ehringhaus, n.d.; White, 2017).

What Is It?

Assessment is always a process, and the summative side of things is no exception. This may seem like a stretch, as a summative assessment feels like the final event in a long series of learning activities and formative assessments. However, keeping in mind that the purpose of assessment is to gather information about student proficiency with the standards in order to make decisions moving forward (Chappuis & Stiggins, 2020; Stiggins, Arter, Chappuis, & Chappuis, 2007), summative assessment is not limited to a traditional test, extended writing assignment, or project. It is also not limited to a single event. Those tasks are key players in determining proficiency, but reassessment to keep improving or to maintain learning is just as important as an event that may be marked as *the* summative assessment. Summative assessment is not time bound to the end of a unit of study, although this may be the most likely timing. Teachers are assessing learning of knowledge and skills in the standards, not students' ability to perform on a specific task type. No matter the task or tasks for summative assessment, it is imperative that alignment to the standards is tight and that teachers have clearly stated the learning outcomes so students can understand and practice them beforehand. Keeping to those requirements focuses learning and assessment throughout the summative process.

Students should never feel that there will be surprises on summative assessments or that they are unsure of how they are going to be assessed. In a truly learning-centered classroom, the teacher makes standards and progressions clear to students and assesses those skills frequently to support learning. Fear and confusion have no role in the summative process. Clarity and alignment place the focus on the demonstration of skills and understanding; teachers are assessing the quality of students' skills and the Depth of Knowledge level of the standard that is being assessed (Webb, 2002).

To dive deeply into summative assessment, we'll first explore the summative paradigm and the ways that summative assessment differs from formative assessment. Then we'll take a look at developing and using summative assessments. After that, we'll spend some time on summative assessment's relationship with grading, including how to understand and use summative assessment results.

The Summative Paradigm

Summative assessment differs from formative assessment in two important ways. The first is how teachers use the assessment data or evidence. In the summative realm, teachers use data and evidence to make a judgment about student proficiency, meaning that they commonly use summative data for grading and reporting (Schimmer et al., 2018). During the summative process, teachers' and students' focus must still be on student learning and demonstration of new skills, even though a grade or score may be tied to that assessment. Maintaining the focus on learning instead of grading becomes increasingly difficult as students get older, but for this type of assessment to fulfill the purpose of providing accurate evidence of learning, it is essential. If students only work for a letter or a number and do not place utmost importance on the skill, learning can be slowed or capped. That is, students may work up to a certain level of achievement and then decide they do not need to learn any more.

Think about a student who is focused on grades. He has determined that he needs to get a B on an assessment in order to maintain his overall grade of A for the marking period. Because of this, the student's primary consideration is how to do just enough for a B. The questions this student asks of his teacher align tightly with this thinking—what the grade will comprise—rather than the learning that will happen and how he will demonstrate it. Even though the standard in this unit has been identified and communicated as a priority, the student may not put in his best effort to achieve mastery because of his focus on doing just enough to keep his A.

The teacher sets the tone for learning and controls the message of what is most important. A teacher's conversations with students regarding summative assessment must always lead with the knowledge, understandings, and skills the students are to demonstrate rather than how the teacher will score an assessment. We do not mean that teachers should ignore explanations of scoring, but teachers should show students that the grade or score is secondary to learning, beginning with the order that they address these two topics. Numbers and letters may be finite, but learning is not.

The second important difference between summative and formative assessment is the depth with which teachers assess a skill or standard. Teachers use summative assessment to determine whether students are proficient with a standard in its entirety, not whether students can achieve mastery of the targets in a learning progression. The two achievements are tied together but different. Progressions are exclusive to the formative side and create the pathway for learning and skill development. As important as it is to deconstruct standards and create progressions, teachers must put those standards back together for summative assessment. A summative assessment should not simply address the series of smaller skills presented throughout a progression. Rather, it should have students demonstrate the larger skill or skills that the standard represents.

Figure 3.1 (page 54) is an example of a high school social studies standard, the summative assessment tied to it, its learning progression, and the formative assessments

Standard: Distinguish between long-term causes and triggering events in developing a historical argument. (D2.His.15.9-12)

Summative Assessment: Write an essay explaining the long-term causes and triggering events that led up to World War I.

Learning Targets	Formative Assessments
Identify triggers leading up to a historical event or time period.	Whole-class reading and discussion Small-group activity (finding trigger events)
Identify causes of a historical event or time period.	Class discussion Journal entry
Explain how causes and triggers impact a historical event or time period.	Individual short written response
Introduce a historical argument.	Modeling by the teacher Graphic organizer Individual practice (writing part of a first draft of the summative assessment) Peer assessment
Support a historical argument with specific claims and evidence.	Modeling by the teacher Graphic organizer Individual practice (writing part of a first draft of the summative assessment) Feedback from the teacher

Opportunities for Reassessment: Revise the writing assignment, incorporating feedback from the teacher.

Source for standard: National Council for the Social Studies, 2017.

FIGURE 3.1: Assessment plan for a standard—Summative assessment and formative assessment alignment to targets.

*Visit **go.SolutionTree.com/assessment** for a free reproducible version of this figure.*

tied to the targets. This assessment plan also leaves space to consider reassessment to preplan for some students who may need additional support, teaching, and practice.

Reassessment is an essential part of planning the summative process. If assessment is the process of learning, a response is necessary when students do not demonstrate proficiency, even with summative assessment. If the classroom is fully focused on learning, teachers and students must take action when students do not demonstrate proficiency. Otherwise, gaps in learning can form, and it becomes acceptable to ignore them. Educators know that small gaps in learning can lead to much larger obstacles, misunderstandings, and consistent errors. As Mike Mattos, Richard DuFour, Rebecca DuFour, Robert Eaker, and Thomas W. Many (2016) put it, "The longer students are allowed to fail, the deeper the academic hole they dig, and the harder it will be to get them out" (p. 113).

Proactively planning for reassessment means preparing for learning to again take center stage. There will be many times that reassessment is already infused in the classroom and curriculum, especially with standards and skills that spiral (ongoing skills that recur in the curriculum) throughout the school year. As a rule of thumb, if the skill will come up and need to be assessed again in a future unit of study, there is no need to pause and address reassessment right away for that skill. A fifth-grade example of this would be, "Quote accurately from a text when explaining what the text says explicitly and when drawing inferences from the text" (RL.5.1; NGA & CCSSO, 2010a). Other times, if the skill is something students will need to master in order to interact with future learning or only comes up once in the curriculum, the reassessment process will need to happen before moving on to new content and skills. A middle school science example of this would be, "Apply Newton's Third Law to design a solution to a problem involving the motion of two colliding objects" (MS-PS2-1; NGSS Lead States, 2013). In this case, teachers can plan for enough time to re-engage learners, provide reteaching and enrichment, and reassess as necessary. Reassessment reinforces student-teacher relationships by promoting the idea of *yet* and reassuring students that everyone is working together toward the same goal. This instills a growth mindset and the idea that learning is never complete (Dweck, 2016).

The Development of Summative Assessment

When designing a summative assessment tool, teachers must take care to provide students ample opportunity to show their proficiency while tightly aligning the tool to the standard. Focusing on the verb or verbs and context in the standard (going back to the process of deconstructing standards from chapter 2, page 29) will drive decisions about the method and delivery of the assessment. For summative assessment to serve its intended purpose, the tool must be valid and reliable. Validity ensures that the assessment tool is accurately gauging proficiency with the standard. Reliability means that teachers are measuring evidence against the standard consistently (Erkens et al., 2017).

There are three types of assessment: (1) selected response, (2) constructed response, and (3) performance based (Chappuis, Stiggins, Arter, & Chappuis, 2004). Each has its own productive use as well as limitations depending on the standard or standards that teachers will assess. *Selected-response* assessments (multiple choice, true/false, matching, and so on) are those that provide students with answer choices. Although it is easier to envision selected response on the formative side when students are building schema to use with higher-order thinking skills, teachers can effectively employ selected response for summative assessment when the skill is of lower complexity. Consider the following kindergarten standard: "Identify whether the number of objects in one group is greater than, less than, or equal to the number of objects in another group" (K.CC.C.6; NGA & CCSSO, 2010b). Since students will be identifying *greater than*, *less than*, or *equal to*, teachers can easily assess this standard with a selected-response assessment in either a written or oral format. The assessment will encompass the entire standard, and teachers can then analyze the evidence to determine proficiency. With selected-response assessment, an appropriate sample size is essential, as students may inadvertently select an incorrect answer even if they have proficiency with the skill. Students can also guess correctly and provide an inaccurate picture of understanding. The sample size will vary and is determined by how much evidence the teacher needs to determine proficiency.

Selected-response assessment tools are not always easy to create, depending on the skills students are to demonstrate. If the standard were "Determine the meaning of words and phrases as they are used in a text, including figurative language such as metaphors and similes" (RL.5.4; NGA & CCSSO, 2010a), the teacher would need to take the time to develop the prompts and questions from a text, and also craft high-quality answer choices. The prompts and questions must be clear, concise, and worded in a way that students can comprehend. When creating answer choices, the teacher should make each choice a viable option. Returning to the purpose of assessment—gathering evidence of student learning—if there is a "throwaway" answer choice, a teacher cannot learn about where students are making mistakes in their thinking if they choose that option. If teachers create the answer choices from common mistakes and misunderstandings, they learn from each answer selection, whether it is right or wrong.

Teachers can address the vast majority of current curricular standards by using constructed-response summative assessment. *Constructed-response* assessments range from short-answer questions to longer responses provided orally or in writing. The key is that the assessment does not present answer choices to students. Rather, students must construct their own responses to a question or prompt. For example, a middle school social studies standard states, "Explain how economic decisions affect the well-being of individuals, businesses, and society" (D2.Eco.1.6-8; National Council for the Social Studies, 2017). With this standard, a few short-answer questions would provide students ample opportunity to show their proficiency.

For so many standards, simply recalling information is not the end goal. The application of that knowledge to show understanding is what enables students to display proficiency with the standards. Verbs such as *analyze, solve, explain, compare, summarize,* and *evaluate* are representative of many standards across the content areas that require more than selected response to capture evidence of student learning. For these and many others, a constructed-response, short-answer assessment is appropriate. Constructed-response assessments have students provide answers that give a window into their thinking, rather than just requiring them to make a selection.

Performance-based assessments align to standards that demand students demonstrate their learning through something like a performance, presentation, or visual representation. These assessment tools usually require a rubric for scoring. Teachers can use performance-based assessments in any content area, but these assessments easily align to the arts, career and technical education, and physical education because of the nature of these content areas' standards. Performance-based assessments many times incorporate a drafting process and are crafted over a period of time with formative assessment and embedded feedback. Although performance-based assessments take the most time for students to complete and the most time for teachers to grade, they provide a substantial amount of learning evidence through one prompt.

For example, a high school chemistry standard states, "Develop models to illustrate the changes in the composition of the nucleus of the atom and the energy released during the processes of fission, fusion, and radioactive decay" (HS-PS1-8; NGSS Lead States, 2013). Since students will have to create a model to prove proficiency with this standard, a performance-based assessment will be necessary. Students can develop this model over time as they learn the content, receive feedback from the teacher, and revise accordingly leading up to their final product.

Figure 3.2 (page 58) is a planning tool for teachers to use with summative assessment. It addresses the essential steps of determining which standard or standards will be assessed, what evidence is necessary to prove proficiency, which assessment type would best correspond to the standards, and what the assessment tool or tools will be. Each of these steps is critical in developing an effective summative assessment process.

Standard or Standards for Summative Assessment:
Evidence of Mastery:
Assessment Type (selected response, constructed response, or performance based):
Assessment Tools:

FIGURE 3.2: Planning tool for summative assessment.

*Visit **go.SolutionTree.com/assessment** for a free reproducible version of this figure.*

Teachers must give careful consideration to developing a summative assessment tool to ensure effectiveness and efficiency. While making sure that the tool is tightly aligned to the standard or standards, teachers must also find the best way to gather evidence of learning (selected response, constructed response, or performance based). Doing this will support a fluid assessment process and allow for timely intervention and reassessment if necessary. Students will get an accurate read on their proficiency, allowing them to be clear on what successes they have had and how they can move forward.

The Use of Summative Assessment

Since teachers use summative assessment to guide decisions and judgments, its role in the classroom differs from that of formative assessment. Teachers use the evidence produced to determine student proficiency as well as to judge the effectiveness of their assessment tools. The way teachers look at that evidence is of critical importance. In order to accurately assess proficiency, teachers must determine success criteria prior to the outset of the unit so they have consistent student expectations. "Success criteria describe in specific terms what successful attainment of the learning goals looks like" (Ontario Ministry of Education, 2010). Inconsistencies in determining what evidence of learning will prove proficiency create different expectations that depend on which teacher students have or which class period they are in.

The way that teachers administer summative assessment also matters. Framing summative assessment as an opportunity to demonstrate learning rather than a moment to fear is of utmost importance. Teachers play a vital role in creating a positive environment for assessment, and the summative paradigm has historically been a source of fear, disengagement, and anxiety for some students (White, 2017). Students understand assessment as a supportive process when teachers present the summative process to them as a time to confidently show what they know, understand, and are able to do. At the same time, students who falter in the summative process know that if the assessment does not go well, they will have another opportunity in the future. Using this process to build student self-efficacy creates a learning-centered environment as well as hopeful students who know that success is on the horizon.

Summative assessment can carry quite a bit of weight in the decision-making process for students. With grades being tied to summative assessment, decisions based on the evidence gathered impact not only day-to-day happenings but also report cards, grade point averages, and future placement of students in varying coursework. Former education professor and author Lorna M. Earl (2013) brings this topic to the forefront in her book *Assessment as Learning*. She writes:

> It [summative assessment] contributes to pivotal decisions that will affect students' futures. It is important, then, that the underlying logic and measurement be credible and defensible and teachers should concentrate on ensuring that they have used assessment to provide accurate and sound statements of proficiency or competence for students. (Earl, 2013, p. 30)

It is important to place this quotation in the context of learning. Proper course placement and decisions about students' futures should maximize learning. As these decisions depend on many things, often including grades, teachers should use summative assessment not only to determine a proficiency level but also to continually improve student learning. The latter is the primary focus.

Summative Assessment and Grading

Grading is tied to summative assessment, and it is important to think about the impact grades and assessment have on each other. Teachers must take care with grading practices to ensure that the evidence they use to make summative judgments about proficiency is accurate. For some standards, this will be the most recent evidence of learning. An example of this would be a world language standard such as, "Learners understand, interpret, and analyze what is heard, read, or viewed on a variety of topics" (Interpretive Communication; American Council on the Teaching of Foreign Languages, n.d.). Students would improve on their ability to interpret language over the course of a unit of study, so the most accurate evidence of learning would be the most recent evidence. Putting old evidence of learning together with current levels (averaging) would not be appropriate, as it would distort the communication of achievement.

Other times, students would need to show a skill multiple times to demonstrate proficiency once they have had ample time to practice and master the standard. An example of this would be a standard such as, "Add and subtract within 20" (1.OA.C; NGA & CCSSO, 2010b). In this case, the frequency with which a student can perform the skill takes the lead. The teacher would want to make sure that a student can accurately produce this fluency multiple times before making a summative judgment and assigning a proficiency level.

Practices like averaging beginning evidence of learning with new evidence after instruction, practice, and formative assessment do not communicate to students that learning is most important. Rather, these practices tell them that they must be proficient with new skills from the outset because even their early mistakes will influence the final grade. Summative assessment data should be the only evidence that determines grades, and new proof of learning must take precedence when teachers have employed reassessment. The purpose of grading is to communicate student proficiency in relation to the standards at a particular moment in time. For teachers to fulfill this purpose, they must take care when crafting summative assessment tools. These tools must provide ample opportunity for students to show their proficiency with the standards. As mentioned, the combination of tight alignment to standards and clear success criteria leads to successful summative assessment, thus leading to accurate grading. An especially important consideration is how to handle results— both understanding them and using them to continue learning.

Understanding Results

In order to produce useful evidence and results from summative assessment, teachers must establish clear success criteria that both students and teachers can easily understand. These criteria can take the form of a rubric, examples of proficient work, or a guide to show with what frequency a student must demonstrate a skill. The bottom line is that students and teachers (as individuals and as members of a team) must understand what high-quality work looks or sounds like.

Just having criteria isn't enough; teachers must consider how others can interpret those criteria. For example, if using a rubric, teachers must establish and then analyze the varying descriptions for proficiency levels to determine what evidence from students would fit each one. Detailed, clear descriptions create consistent interpretations of student work aligned to proficiency levels. Students can also play a role with this interpretation. An example of this would be teachers' requiring students to reflect on their performance prior to submitting their final summative work. Having clear success criteria to work with and learn about throughout the course of a unit of study allows students to self-assess to gauge their proficiency. With this, teachers and students can collaboratively plan for future learning. However, teachers must always maintain the leadership role in the classroom. There will be times when students do not accurately interpret their assessment results and need support moving forward. Like any skill, self-assessment will improve over time with practice for students and guidance from teachers. Figure 3.3 is an example rubric for a high school science class.

Conduct an investigation or test design.			
4	3	2	1
Uses appropriate scientific methods and systematically collects multiple trials (if appropriate) of relevant data consistent within a narrow range Evaluates the consistency of the data as well as the appropriateness of the data collection procedures	Uses appropriate scientific methods and systematically collects multiple trials (if appropriate) of relevant data consistent within a reasonable range Evaluates the consistency (precision) of the data	Uses appropriate scientific methods and collects multiple trials (if appropriate) of relevant data consistent within a reasonable range	Uses appropriate scientific methods and collects multiple trials (if appropriate) of relevant data, but the data are not consistent within a reasonable range

Source for rubric: Literacy Design Collaborative, 2018.

FIGURE 3.3: Example rubric.

The skill figure 3.3 represents is one students can apply in multiple areas of science as well as at multiple grade levels. The four levels lay out descriptors of the quality of work students should demonstrate but are still open for interpretation from students and teachers. Teachers must discuss how to determine what evidence would meet these criteria; simply crafting a rubric does not ensure inter-rater reliability among teachers. Examining student work samples along with the rubric guides decisions about acceptable evidence for proficiency and has value when explaining the different levels to students.

Using Results to Continue Learning

Communication of assessment results is sometimes limited to a letter or number in the eyes of students and teachers. While providing letters and numbers will continue for the foreseeable future, what those communicate and how they are interpreted require close attention. It is commonly understood that an A represents a high level of achievement, but what does that mean for student learning? Alongside those letters and numbers that traditionally appear with summative assessment, there is also room for teachers to describe what each proficiency level (represented by the letter or number) means as well as provide feedback. Providing these descriptions and feedback will support the focus on learning and skill development. Chapter 4 (page 73) will more fully examine feedback. Traditionally, students and teachers have seen the letters and numbers as an end point, and it will take work on the part of educators to honor those as markers of current proficiency while communicating what they mean for future learning.

When results are accurately communicated in a timely fashion to students, they can serve as a springboard for learning. If students are highly proficient at the end of a unit, they should feel confident that their success will continue moving forward. Their proficient result should motivate students and build hope. For students who are not yet proficient, teachers can create this same hope with sound re-engagement, relearning, and reassessment practices.

Learning for Teachers

It cannot be overstated how much teachers learn through the summative assessment process. From developing assessment tools to administrating the assessment, and finally analyzing the results, they learn at every phase. Traditionally, with summative assessment, teachers have mainly focused on the evidence of learning that they gather from students. While this is still very important, we also want to point out that teachers gain so much more from the summative assessment process than just the end product.

Since teachers begin with the end in mind, "A good learning outcome must be measurable, such that serious thought about summative assessment is needed at the start of the planning process" (Kibble, 2017, p. 111). When designing summative assessment tools, teachers must dive deeply into what their standards mean and demand from students. Then, each time they teach, practice, and assess a standard within one school year or from year to year, teachers' learning increases. This learning allows teachers to reflect to improve instruction and assessment practices in future years, while also considering the many variables that influence student learning. Students are different from year to year. Demands on the day-to-day schedule often change, and the best-laid plans will inevitably have to change from time to time. Increased knowledge of standards allows teachers to improve their summative assessment process and to be prepared to pivot when necessary.

When administering summative assessments, teachers learn about their students and how they experience those moments of assessment. With a traditional test, teachers may learn that certain students thrive with this type of assessment, while for others, it is a very anxious event. The same can be true for other assessment types. Some students are fearful of a long-term, multistep project, and still others do very well with an extended writing assignment. The teacher certainly does not have to cater to each student and provide students with their preferred method of assessment every time. For some standards, changing the assessment method would not be appropriate. However, there will also be times when the teacher can provide options to students. Knowing which students will likely be anxious about a certain type of assessment helps the teacher calm some fears before they manifest or as they happen. Teachers can provide students scaffolding for large projects or chunk test items to decrease anxiety about a longer assessment. If teachers show care and are straightforward with learners about their assessment methods and the reasons for them, they can sustain student-teacher relationships.

Before moving on after a summative assessment, teachers must thoroughly analyze student results to truly gauge proficiency. The value of the information gathered for each student is obvious, but teachers need to evaluate the validity of that information as well. Many times, teachers see results that confirm what they predicted about student achievement. Other times, there is a mismatch, which teachers cannot ignore. If a student has shown increased knowledge, understanding, and skill throughout a unit and, all of a sudden, this student does not perform on the summative assessment, or vice versa, the teacher needs to do some investigating to uncover why this happened. This learning for teachers is ongoing. Acting on the information they gather allows them to support resilience and academic achievement for students.

Figure 3.4 (page 64) provides some reflection questions for teachers or teacher teams to use after administering a summative assessment. These questions support continual learning for teachers and provide guidance to improve the summative process as well as the development and revision of the assessment tools.

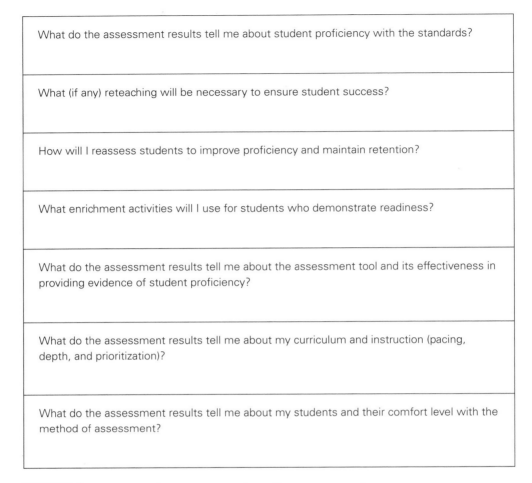

What do the assessment results tell me about student proficiency with the standards?

What (if any) reteaching will be necessary to ensure student success?

How will I reassess students to improve proficiency and maintain retention?

What enrichment activities will I use for students who demonstrate readiness?

What do the assessment results tell me about the assessment tool and its effectiveness in providing evidence of student proficiency?

What do the assessment results tell me about my curriculum and instruction (pacing, depth, and prioritization)?

What do the assessment results tell me about my students and their comfort level with the method of assessment?

FIGURE 3.4: Teacher reflection questions for a summative assessment.

*Visit **go.SolutionTree.com/assessment** for a free reproducible version of this figure.*

A final piece of learning for teachers is the opportunity to reflect on their learning progressions. Once they have received summative evidence and data, teachers can reflect on the flow of the unit as a whole. How did the progressions work for students? How did the progressions support their teaching? Are there any tweaks or changes that could increase the progressions' usefulness? These reflections are most impactful immediately after the summative process, and teachers should note any changes at that time. Otherwise, reflection at the end of a school year for a unit in the first marking period can be inaccurate. Noting changes to make for the next year throughout the current year allows for teachers to continuously learn and make accurate reflections about their learning progressions.

Learning for Students

Through summative assessment, students learn (and hopefully confirm) what they know about their own proficiency with the standards they have been working on throughout a unit of study. Students should develop confidence that they are ready for what is to come and prepared to rely on their understanding and skill development as a foundation to build on.

At the summative level, reflection creates learning for students. Error analysis is an important part of this reflection—it will inform students and teachers of any small mistakes or larger misunderstandings that students may still have and that will require continued learning or reassessment. Figure 3.5 provides an example error-analysis form for a traditional test.

Item Number	Correct or incorrect?	If incorrect, is it a minor mistake or large misunderstanding?	If incorrect, what are your next steps?
1			
2			
3			
4			

FIGURE 3.5: Error-analysis tool.

*Visit **go.SolutionTree.com/assessment** for a free reproducible version of this figure.*

For a performance-based assessment, a similar reflection or analysis would be very beneficial, but the format would differ. Many times, a performance-based assessment has students apply several standards at the same time, so breaking down the skills into those that students indicate as mastered and those that they indicate as still needing work gets a little muddy. In this case, the teacher can list the skills for reflection or use a rubric to break down the skills for the students; this will create a more accurate reflection that yields key information on specific skills to use moving forward. A single-point rubric such as the one represented in figure 3.6 (page 66) can be helpful for this, no matter whether the teacher is assessing several standards or a single standard with multiple skills.

Standard: With some guidance and support from adults, use technology, including the internet, to produce and publish writing as well as to interact and collaborate with others. (W.5.6)		
Areas for Growth	Proficiency	Evidence of Mastery
	I can produce writing on my topic. I can publish my writing using technology. I can interact and collaborate with my peers to provide feedback and revise my writing.	

Standard: Conduct short research projects that use several sources to build knowledge through investigation of different aspects of a topic. (W.5.7)		
Areas for Growth	Proficiency	Evidence of Mastery
	I can choose a topic for research. I can find sources to build knowledge on a topic. I can use several sources to build knowledge on several aspects of a topic.	
Teacher Comments:		
Student Comments:		

Source for standards: NGA & CCSSO, 2010a.

FIGURE 3.6: Single-point rubric.

*Visit **go.SolutionTree.com/assessment** for a free reproducible version of this figure.*

In this example, students are to research a topic of their choosing using several sources to build their knowledge and then produce writing to demonstrate that knowledge. They publish the writing on a digital platform; the teacher asks students to provide feedback to their peers, and then students revise their work accordingly. Students can self-assess against the rubric, identifying skills with which they feel they are proficient (and noting evidence of mastery) while making note of skills where they need continued learning and growth.

Summative assessment is also an opportunity for students to pause and analyze how their learning has progressed. They can reflect on which styles of instruction and practice worked for them and which ones potentially did not. Students and teachers monitor this throughout the formative process, but a more global reflection at the end of a unit is also very beneficial. Figure 3.7 shows a sample form that students could use for reflection and teachers could use for analysis for future planning.

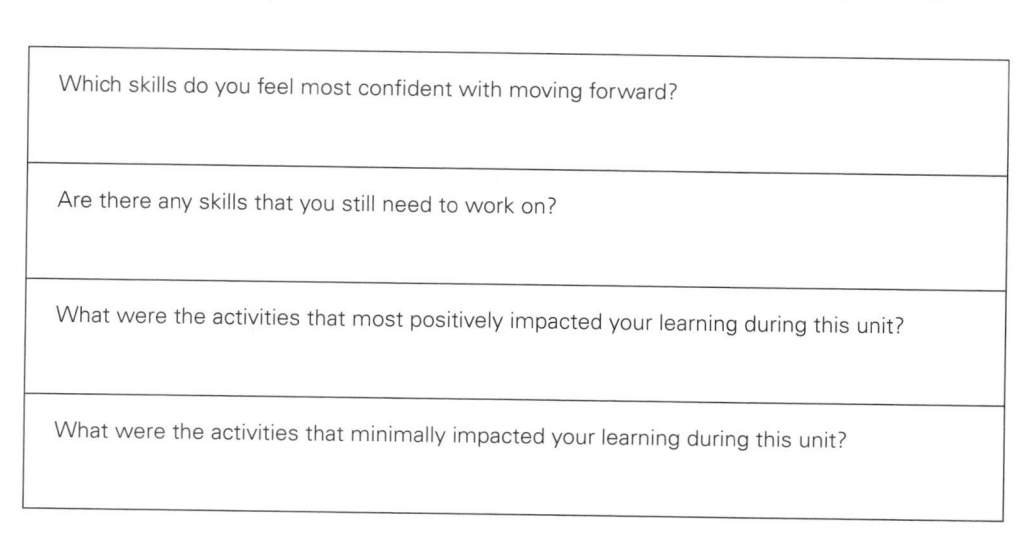

Which skills do you feel most confident with moving forward?

Are there any skills that you still need to work on?

What were the activities that most positively impacted your learning during this unit?

What were the activities that minimally impacted your learning during this unit?

FIGURE 3.7: Student reflection questions for a summative assessment.

Visit **go.SolutionTree.com/assessment** *for a free reproducible version of this figure.*

When students use summative assessment and data to identify any areas for growth, they are better prepared to take action. They have clarity surrounding the specific skills that need additional teaching, practice, and eventual reassessment. Many times with traditional assessment practices, it is unclear where students specifically need to improve. They may know the assessment did not go well, but when teachers employ summative assessment effectively, students should be able to easily see their areas of strength and areas for growth. Students can use this information to concisely self-advocate and move forward with their learning.

Summative assessment can play a strong role in the PLC process. Teachers can collaborate to make sure all students realize this growth.

Collaboration Around Assessment

The three big ideas of a PLC are all in play with summative assessment. Clearly, being results oriented is an essential piece. But when used effectively, summative assessment is also a way for teams to focus on learning and realize a collaborative culture. Teachers want all students to achieve at high levels. If the intended outcome of a sound assessment system is to create hopeful students who believe in themselves and in turn achieve, summative assessment must play a contributing role. Teachers must perform a balancing act to remind students that a summative assessment is a culmination of a unit but that learning never ceases. The focus on results centers on which skills students have learned and demonstrated, not how many questions they got right or points they accrued. The collaboration that occurs around these results is critical.

While learning progressions (chapter 2, page 29) focus on critical question 1 (What do students need to know and be able to do?) and support critical question 2 (How will we know when they have learned it?), summative assessment squarely fits into the latter with verification of learning (DuFour et al., 2016). Critical questions 3 and 4 relate to the formative paradigm when teachers are ready to intervene with students who need additional scaffolding or enrichment. These questions will be addressed in chapters 4 (page 73) and 5 (page 91).

Summative assessment tools do not have to be consistent from teacher to teacher, although they can be. Determining when to use common summative assessments is a choice for teacher teams. What is not a choice is the evidence teachers will accept as proficient for the priority standards they are assessing. The team as a whole can analyze evidence of learning that teachers gather through summative assessment, no matter whether the team members employ a common assessment or create their own summative events. Teachers can still work together to analyze the evidence of learning, reflect on their teaching throughout the unit, and plan how to move forward. The consistency with which teachers discuss standards, evidence of mastery, assessment tools, and student work correlates to their consistency in expectations for students.

Teacher teams can collaborate to maximize student growth by putting into action a process to reassess students. By reassessing students, teachers communicate to them that the focus truly is on learning—if they haven't learned it yet, they *will*. The focus on learning through summative assessment plays directly into the collaborative culture. Collaborative teams can collectively discuss how to go about reassessment with their students and put learning at the forefront of the process. The purpose of reassessment must be to increase learning and proficiency; it must not be for students to see what is on the test or try to play the system with a redo. "With well-crafted assessment tools, students will not be able to do something as simple as memorize answers from the previous assessment to improve their score" (Schimmer et al., 2018, p. 158).

Working together to create a reassessment system is valuable, illuminating work. It involves establishing a purpose as well as developing tools and ideas to use when the time comes to reassess students. When teachers work together to establish reteaching, relearning, and reassessment, the process also becomes more manageable, as teachers on teams share the responsibility to all students. As essential components of the assessment process, accurate interpretation and communication of results have their own focus on learning. With these components in place, students and teachers have a consistent understanding of what a summative assessment will expect and what the assessment's results mean for future growth.

Questions for *Reflection*

*Use these questions to reflect on this chapter's
learning and begin to look forward.*

1. Are our summative assessment tools aligned to the standards?

2. Do we design our summative assessment tools in advance of the unit of study to ensure teachers have a common understanding of the intended learning?

3. Does our team have a common understanding of what proficiency with the standards looks or sounds like to ensure accurate grading?

4. Does our process of scoring summative assessments provide a clear picture of student proficiency with the standards?

5. Are we using the data gathered from summative assessment as a team to learn not only about student proficiency but also about our students and our teaching?

6. Do we have an established process for reassessment? If so, does it maximize student learning?

Next Steps for Determining Summative Assessments

Analyze current summative assessment processes for effectiveness and efficiency.

Revise assessment tools as necessary to ensure alignment with priority standards so students can produce high-quality evidence of learning.

Create new assessment tools as necessary for any priority standards that have not been addressed by summative assessment in the past.

Create or revise rubrics or scoring guides to support accurate interpretation of results for students and teachers.

Employ scoring and grading practices that support further learning and progress.

Prepare for reassessment processes to maximize student confidence and learning.

INFORMAL FORMATIVE ASSESSMENT

For assessment to function
formatively, the results have to be
used to adjust teaching and learning.

—*Paul Black & Dylan Wiliam*

Every moment in the classroom provides an opportunity to learn, whether that be about learning styles, misconceptions, or immediate needs. This chapter addresses assessment as informal interactions and activities and looks at how to make instructional decisions based on in-the-moment data through formative assessment in the form of practice, observations, and conversations. Informal formative assessment is about being mindful and intentional in everyday interactions with students to observe, reflect, provide feedback, and plan with a focus on next steps for instruction. These formative moments are chances to learn—both for teachers and for learners.

What Is It?

Formative assessment does not necessitate a formal event or a stop to teaching and learning. Instead, formative assessment can be an unobtrusive instructional support that facilitates ongoing learning. As defined in chapter 1 (page 7), what makes an assessment formative in nature is the instructional response that occurs in acknowledgment of the data teachers have observed or collected. We intentionally divided chapters 4 (page 73) and 5 (page 91) into two types of formative assessment— (1) informal formative assessment and (2) formal formative assessment—to make an important distinction between the more unobtrusive and the more obtrusive ways that teachers can use formative assessment in the classroom to increase learning for all. Recall our method of distinguishing between these two types; think of them as *formative assessment* (informal) and *Formative assessment* (formal). While teachers can intentionally plan more obtrusive events throughout a learning progression to check on student understanding, plan responses, and ensure readiness with content (formal formative assessment), this chapter sheds light on the more unobtrusive formative assessment methods that are embedded into everyday instruction for the purpose of student-centered decision making.

Every moment during instruction is an opportunity to observe, formatively assess, and employ instructional agility based on observational data. The intentional use of informal assessment repurposes the everyday classroom to allow for meaningful assessment, responses, and learning. This chapter addresses making instructional decisions based on real-time evidence and data through intentional activities, practice, observations, and conversations. Remember to think of informal assessment as formative with a lowercase *f* to emphasize the more informal opportunities to engage and respond to students in an unobtrusive and meaningful way.

Intentionally designing activities and assessments to use formatively does not necessitate overhauling present teaching practices. In fact, the hope is that this chapter celebrates many of the formative assessment methods teachers use and highlights their powerful impact on student learning. We designed this chapter to encourage teachers to focus less on the activity or method itself and more on the student-centered instructional response to ensure learning for all. Through the process of creating learning progressions, teachers should have already discussed and explored the question, What does proficiency look like? With the understanding of proficiency and the steps it will take to get there (outlined through the progression), teachers are prepared to use formative assessment to answer the questions, How will I respond if students are not at proficiency? and How will I respond if students are already proficient? First we'll discuss the purpose and design of effective feedback and then move on to how to develop high-quality informal formative assessment practices.

The Need for Feedback

Educational research continues to show that teaching less and providing more feedback greatly improves student performance and learning (Bransford, Brown, & Cocking, 2000; Dean, Hubbell, Pitler, & Stone, 2012; Hattie, 2009; Marzano, Pickering, & Pollock, 2001). Of course, teaching less does not mean that the teacher is addressing fewer standards or expecting less proficiency. It refers to making the transition from a teacher-centered to a student-centered classroom and focusing instructional decisions on current needs. It means that the teacher is spending less time teaching to the students and more time observing, working with, and responding to students. It is more *learning* instead of more *teaching*. Teaching less puts students at the center of the learning experience and communicates that the teacher is focused not on the product but instead on the process of learning and coaching along the way. Intentional feedback and meaningful interactions ensure that teachers make instructional decisions around what students need and how they will meet those needs.

Research has shown that students perceive feedback in a more positive light when, in addition to judging their work, it fosters meaningful dialogue (Beaumont, O'Doherty, & Shannon, 2011). When teachers deliver feedback orally, conversations naturally emerge that support learners as individuals in a timely and personal way. Infusing formative assessment into daily experiences allows space for these conversations and adds to a learning-centered culture. The role of the teacher is not to be the center of the learning experience and deliver content, but to be a facilitator and coach to encourage and push students to the next level.

Outlining priority standards and learning progressions in advance of a unit ensures consistency, while formative assessment and response, both with instruction and with feedback, provide for an autonomous, student-centered experience. Teachers have the knowledge and confidence to stray from original plans because when they are employing formative assessment measures, they recognize the emerging needs of students. Having the common destination and learning journey outlined through the progression keeps feedback goal oriented and allows for teachers to meet students at their current level.

The Design of Formative Feedback

The *use* of formative assessment results is fundamental to narrowing the gap between where students are and where they need to be. The unpredictability of how and when students learn makes feedback essential to effective learning and improvement (Wiliam, 2013). Understanding how and when to provide feedback is necessary in order for all students to receive the coaching that they need when they need it.

The research on feedback is robust; one common theme is that the effectiveness of feedback is measured by the response it triggers in learners (Hattie & Timperley, 2007; Ruiz-Primo & Li, 2013). That is, what makes feedback effective is the productive response on the part of learners and how they engage with and use that feedback to strengthen their understanding. Many valuable, practical feedback strategies exist (Hillman & Stalets, 2019), but for the purpose of delivering feedback in the informal formative realm and promoting learning conversations between students and teachers, there are three non-negotiable elements of high-quality formative feedback: (1) begin by commenting on the strength of the demonstrated skill, (2) connect that skill to the learning target or standard, and (3) clearly communicate next steps to the learner.

We will discuss each, as well as what high-quality formative feedback looks like in action, in the following sections.

Comment on the Strength of the Demonstrated Skill

By nature, people are more open to receiving constructive feedback when the person providing the feedback recognizes a strength in their work and builds off it (Erkens, Schimmer, & Dimich, 2018). Erkens and colleagues (2018) point out, "The best feedback describes evidenced strengths so the receiver can understand how to maintain good work and then provides a question or a step forward" (p. 153). When delivering feedback to students, a teacher should look for what learners did well and let them know about it. This communicates where they are finding success before moving on to how they should improve their work. It sets the foundation for improvement while letting students know that teachers value their work and efforts. Recognizing the learner's starting place (or location on the learning progression) allows the teacher to design next steps that are aligned, manageable, and attainable.

Connect the Skill to the Current Learning Target or Standard

Learners must understand why the feedback they are receiving is important and how it will get them closer to proficiency with the standard or learning target. Once they recognize a strength, teachers should relate the students' place in learning back to the intended target and discuss what is missing and why continuing their work is important. This will provide learners with direction and purpose while reminding them of their goal.

Clearly Communicate Next Steps to the Learner

Once students understand the strength in their work and are reminded of the intended learning target, it is time for teachers and students to look forward and plan next steps together. Including the words *next*, *to improve*, and *now* in this step in the feedback process helps encourage students to look forward. This can guarantee that as students begin to act on the feedback, they clearly understand the work that they need to do to improve their product and understanding. It is essential to allow time for the student to respond and provide self-assessment to honor the fact that feedback is a conversation.

High-Quality Formative Feedback in Action

This feedback structure does not overwhelm struggling learners or underwhelm advanced learners, but it ensures that each student is receiving the same amount of feedback. It allows feedback to be quick and effective while providing learners with a clear next step to grow in their understanding. It focuses not on what was but on what could and will be. In essence, it should allow learners to see themselves advancing through the learning progression. We recommend using this structure for feedback in an informal setting, such as during a conference, at a student's desk, or even in a quick conversation as a student enters the classroom.

Imagine that during a formative activity, a second-grade class is completing a writing prompt addressing the following standard: "Write narratives in which they recount a well-elaborated event or short sequence of events, include details to describe actions, thoughts, and feelings, use temporal words to signal event order, and provide a sense of closure" (W.2.3; NGA & CCSSO, 2010a). When conferencing with students, the teacher notices that one student has written all about her experience visiting cousins over the weekend but hasn't described her thoughts, feelings, or reactions to the experience. The teacher says:

> Wow! I really like your details on your visit to your cousins' house. Building Legos, playing outside, and having a little bit of time to play video games sounds awesome! Did you enjoy it? Remember that I also want you to talk about how you felt about your time together. When you get back to writing, can you please add some detail to your feelings about your time together?

The teacher then allows time for the student to provide an initial response to the feedback and any additional self-reflection, and then sends her on her way to improve her writing. While this feedback is personalized and provides next steps for this student, the entire encounter is brief, and the student now understands what she has done well and what comes next.

When continuing to observe the class and conference, the teacher reads the work of another student, who has already shown proficiency with the standard. The teacher says:

> I really enjoy reading about your experience with baseball. I feel like I am at your practice and can feel your love for the game. You've communicated order through your use of *next* and *then* and *finally*. To continue to improve your writing, I'd like to challenge you to elaborate when it comes to the setting. Can you describe where you are and what it feels like to be there?

Again, the teacher then allows time for the student to provide an initial response to the feedback and any additional self-reflection, and then sends the student on his way to improve his writing.

When responding to the needs of learners and delivering effective feedback, it is critical to consider the question, Who is doing the thinking? As students get older, or as they increase in proficiency, it is appropriate to hand some of the responsibility of designing next steps to them. After teachers have observed work and communicated strengths to students, they can ask, "Have you identified any areas that need improvement that I can help you with?" or "When reviewing the success criteria, can you identify anything that needs improvement?" The teacher can still provide additional feedback after this interaction, but involving students in the conversation strengthens their ownership and self-awareness of their learning. Structuring classroom activities to include these conversations grants time for the teacher to be responsive and provide individualized feedback.

The Design of Informal Formative Assessment

Teachers can use many methods to repurpose classroom activities and instructional tools to make them formative in nature and allow time for effective feedback and conversations centered on learning. The following sections highlight some suggestions for how teachers can use several classroom activities to create a learner-centered experience and allow for a greater and more intentional instructional response.

Observation

The more teachers know about students, the more they can plan to help them. Observation is arguably one of the most effective informal formative assessment tools that teachers have at their disposal because it is ongoing and always available (White, 2016). With observation, teachers can watch for frustration (Is the learner not yet proficient enough to work independently?), confidence (Is the learner finding success?), boredom (Is the learner not being challenged?), or common misunderstandings (Do I need to reteach to a small group?). The observation process creates a transition in learning experiences, putting the heavy lifting in the hands of the learners while the teacher gets a chance to work with, observe, and respond to different learners. Often, this means altering intended plans and instead providing timely, personalized responses to attend to the messages, both verbal and nonverbal, that students are sending about their journey toward proficiency. When observing, consider the following questions.

- What are you learning about how students are responding to your instruction?

- How do you know when students are hitting the target? What does their learning look like?

- What are you listening for? What does non-learning look and sound like?

- How are students engaging with the content? How do you respond when they do not engage?

- How well are students able to communicate the degree to which they are learning? How are you providing them the opportunity to communicate their learning?

Observation goes beyond watching students work and providing feedback. It includes understanding students' learning styles, knowing what their reactions mean for future instruction, and planning how to personalize the learning process. Using a student observation tool such as the one shown in figure 4.1 can prove helpful.

Learning Progression	Notes of Student Needs	Intervention Ideas
Learning target 1:		
Learning target 2:		
Learning target 3:		
Learning target 4:		

FIGURE 4.1: Student observation template.

*Visit **go.SolutionTree.com/assessment** for a free reproducible version of this figure.*

Teachers can keep this tool on a clipboard as they walk around, observe, and provide feedback to keep note of misunderstandings, concerns, or enrichment needs. This is not meant to be time-consuming or overwhelming but more of a tool to quickly take notes to reference later. Teachers can use this to create groupings and intentionally design activities around student needs for the next class period or school day. There is flexibility in the use of this tool, but its primary purpose is the intentional gathering of observational data for targeted future instruction. For example, under Notes of Student Needs, teachers could indicate students for future grouping, emerging themes, or areas for whole-group reteaching.

Think-Pair-Share

While the role of the teacher during think-pair-share is primarily observation, this method provides a perfect opportunity to collect informal formative data and exercise instructional agility in the middle of a lesson. When teachers need to do a quick check on classroom understanding to see student thoughts on a target, they can provide learners a couple of minutes to gather their thoughts and share them with a partner. During this time, the teacher walks around and listens to the conversations. Teachers can add prompts to the assessment by asking, "Who can share something new they learned from their partner?" or "What is a question you and your partner are still challenged by?" During this quick assessment, teachers grant themselves the time to check students' communication of understanding, both verbal and nonverbal. In response, teachers model flexibility and responsiveness as they address any emerging needs before moving on with instruction.

Conferencing

Whether a classroom uses a workshop model or a more traditional setting, conferencing can be an effective formative assessment tool. Conferencing involves building in time to meet with students to focus on learning and *specific* needs. It allows the teacher to collect informal formative data about the needs of individuals, as well as the class, to ensure that next steps meet those needs. It is ideal to conduct individual conferences; however, teachers can also conference with students in small groups. No matter the format, it is essential to listen and provide pinpointed recommendations for improvement. While conferencing with students is a significant time investment, the information teachers can glean from them is invaluable.

The following are some recommendations for effective conferencing in the classroom.

- **Start conferencing early in the year:** Begin to set the norm in the first week or two of school. This helps develop an independent learning culture and allows teachers to form strong relationships and trust with students.

- **Teach students how to prepare for a conference:** Inform them of what work they should bring, what types of questions they should ask, whether they should be prepared with a self-assessment of their work, and whether they should bring their learning progressions to guide the conversation and assessment.

- **Prepare ahead of time for conferences:** Review student work or reference an observational tool such as figure 4.1 (page 79), and plan a few questions to ask each learner. Use a log or running record to organize observations and student needs.

- **Plan for individual instructional responses:** Consider what students' immediate next steps and takeaways should be. What should students work on when they walk away from the conference?

- **Plan the whole-group instructional response after conferencing:**
  Determine whether the whole class shares certain needs. Are there any
  topics that should be retaught? How can groups be formed based on
  conference observations?

Jan Chappuis (2015) has introduced the three-minute conference to allow the
teacher to quickly and effectively work with each learner. While teachers might
be concerned about how long conferences should take or how long to meet with
each student, this structure allows the process to be efficient and meaningful. The
structure of a three-minute conference is as follows.

- **Minute 1:** Students provide a self-assessment of their work. They share
  strengths, weaknesses, and overall reactions to their readiness and
  understanding.

- **Minute 2:** The teacher adds to the conversation by honoring the
  students' self-assessment and adding on any other strengths and areas
  that need strengthening.

- **Minute 3:** Together, students and teacher develop a plan for
  improvement. Depending on students' age and experience, this is
  another opportunity to let students guide discussion and design next
  steps in their learning.

Four Corners

There are many variations of the four corners activity, but this section highlights
one method and its use as an informal formative assessment tool. A teacher outlines
four learning targets that address proficiency with the standard for a unit and assigns
one target to each corner of the classroom. The teacher discusses the four targets
and asks students to each go to the corner of the room (premarked) that represents
the target they are struggling with the most. In that corner, students have three
minutes to work with their peers and come up with a list of questions they have
about the target. The teachers may provide sentence starters such as, "What if . . ."
or "I'm confused when . . ." Then the teacher goes corner to corner, asking students
to share one of their questions with the class. After they share a question, the other
corners conference on their response (with the teacher observing) and share out or
use whiteboards to model their thoughts.

Teachers can use this activity formatively as they actively observe and respond
when the students ask and answer questions. Students are involved in the learning
process, and all responses from the teacher center on the emerging needs of learners.
This is a student-led activity, but teachers are actively watching for moments when

they can provide clarification or ask an additional question of learners. Teachers can also use this observation to plan future instruction and provide on-the-spot feedback.

Warm-Ups

When designing warm-ups, also known as *do-nows* or *bell ringers*, teachers must intentionally allow for a formative response. Teachers must be purposeful about what is included, whether that be checking on retention of a previously taught skill or having repetition with a skill that has proven to be challenging. Through warm-ups, teachers can collect data and respond to emerging themes that require more time to learn in a meaningful manner. Warm-ups are opportune moments to formatively assess, discuss common misconceptions, and use observational strategies. While it is challenging, teachers should avoid using the warm-up as a classroom management tool to take attendance and do housekeeping, and should instead dive into student work. Following are some suggestions for using warm-ups as informal formative assessment tools.

- **Do not grade warm-ups:** Grading warm-ups will discourage vulnerability and a willingness to ask questions during the process. Teachers need not expect proficiency; the priority lies in engagement, instructional response, and increased learning. Students must understand this goal so that they enter the experience with a growth mindset and an understanding that teachers expect mistakes.

- **Develop a routine that lets students know the purpose of warm-ups:** Students should know what types of activities teachers will use for warm-ups, how they can organize their work samples, how much time they will have to work on them, and how teachers will interact with learners. This teaches students to engage in the process and develop routines.

- **Be prepared to meet students where they are:** Teachers should provide an environment where each learner has the chance to grow. Since warm-ups are intentionally planned around student needs, teachers must make sure that each learner is receiving coaching during this time.

As an example, consider a primary classroom that is working on sentence structure. Since this is an ongoing skill throughout the school year, the teacher uses a journal to monitor growth and encourage reflection. There is an anchor chart displayed at the front of the classroom highlighting how to compose a sentence. As students enter the classroom, they see a sentence starter on the board stating, "I feel . . ." and students know to begin their writing in their journals. As they write, the teacher monitors and provides guidance, and as soon as students are done, he goes through the anchor chart with a focus on what he has observed. After noticing several students forgetting punctuation at the end of their sentences, he writes his sentence at the board, intentionally leaving off punctuation. He asks students to provide him feedback and asks them to correct the sentence. This student-centered response makes the warm-up formative in nature.

Marker Boards

Marker boards or dry-erase boards (or a digital equivalent) are a classroom resource that teachers can use to quickly observe student work and understanding. This method affords each student a space to respond; teachers can formatively assess the classroom in an informal way without much preparation or planning. If a teacher wants to take a moment to scan the understanding and needs of the classroom, marker boards provide a way to engage in a quick and easy assessment of student learning.

When using these tools with a formative purpose, it is necessary to anticipate misconceptions and plan the instructional response. For example, consider a high school mathematics teacher checking students' understanding of triangle congruence by using marker boards. Anticipating a common misconception, the teacher places two triangles on display that cannot be determined to be congruent. When scanning the room, the teacher notices that three partner pairs have the same incorrect answer. Instead of isolating those students, the teacher says:

> I'd like you to pay attention to the incorrect answer I'm about to put up on the board. This is a very common mistake, so I'd like to talk about it as a class. What advice would you give a peer who provided this answer? What misunderstanding is shown?

The teacher jots down this problem area in order to remember to use a similar example in the next day's warm-up to readdress this common concern. This wasn't planned, but the response was necessary based on observational evidence. This instructional response makes the marker board activity formative in nature.

Learning for Teachers

According to education professor and researcher Patrick Griffin (2007), teachers acquire evidence of learning through what students say, write, make, or do; these student actions potentially provide teachers with the necessary indicators to accurately infer the students' current learning status. When the role of classroom activities evolves to formative assessment experiences, the activities change from looking at *what was* to looking at *what could and will be*. This evolution instills in teachers and students the understanding that each moment in the classroom is an opportunity to learn, assess, and respond. Learners develop the belief that they will succeed and that they can trust their teacher. Informal formative assessment shifts the classroom focus from the activity itself to the learning that happens from the activity.

Informal formative assessment provides a unique opportunity to look at the *whole learner*, meaning how students learn, what they know, and what they need. In order to maximize learning through the informal formative process, teachers can make simple changes to their communication with learners. Beyond observing learning needs, teachers can use the following questions for everyday individual discussions to increase their knowledge about learners.

- "How is learning going for you today? Do you need anything additional from me?"

- "I noticed through your body language that this content might be challenging you. Can I answer any questions for you?"

- "I noticed through your body language that this content might not be challenging you. Can I provide you with a different learning experience?"

- "What challenges you the most? What is the easiest for you?"

- "Do you have any feedback for me?"

The interaction between teacher and students has been characterized as a principal source of evidence in formative assessment (Heritage, 2013), so whether the student is *saying, writing, making,* or *doing,* it is the interaction that is most revealing. The process of collecting and acting on this evidence is where the learning happens for teachers and where they can form and strengthen relationships.

Research continues to show that students' confidence and efficacy increase when they receive feedback that is positive and reflective (Jung, Diefes-Dux, Horvath, Rodgers, & Cardella, 2015). So it is imperative that as teachers engage in the process of formative assessment and feedback, they keep the focus on recognizing and praising strengths and effort, relating feedback back to the target, and providing steps to move forward in learning.

Learning for Students

Infusing formative assessment, effective feedback, and instructional responses tailored to students' needs into everyday classroom experiences increases learning for students because they receive information about where they are in their progression and what comes next. It allows for more conversations between teacher and learner, which leads to deeper student engagement.

Allowing this coaching to happen during the school day increases learners' motivation and confidence as they receive feedback and next steps for improvement. Students can use tools such as figure 4.2 to take note of feedback they receive in order to organize their learning and progress.

Feedback Journal		
Learning Targets	Feedback I Received	Mastery Reached? (Write yes or no.)
Name, graph, and describe the location of ordered pairs on the coordinate plane.		Yes!
Develop and apply the formula for midpoint.	Remember to check the midpoint's location on the graph to make sure it looks like the middle.	Yes!
Use the distance formula, the Pythagorean theorem, or both to find the distance between two points.	If the points form a vertical or horizontal line, I can just count the distance. Make sure to form a right triangle. $(x - x)^2$ is similar to a^2 because they are both finding the horizontal distance.	

FIGURE 4.2: Student feedback reflection.

*Visit **go.SolutionTree.com/assessment** for a free reproducible version of this figure.*

In this example, the teacher has communicated the learning progression and targets to students and provided them a document to record any feedback or misconceptions they encounter; the document also includes a column to record when they have mastered the targets. Note that this is an ongoing tool. The feedback box for the first target is blank because the learner showed early mastery that did not require feedback. The mastery column for the third target is blank because the student has not achieved mastery yet.

Engaging in informal formative assessment and feedback grants students the ability to receive instruction and conversation tailored to their needs. This is a time for students to learn about not only what they know but also how to invest in their learning.

Though informal formative assessment leaves space for individual teachers to follow their instructional instincts, collaboration in this area is highly beneficial.

Collaboration Around Assessment

When teachers couple formative assessment with everyday instruction, they can easily focus on learning and results. The process of *teaching* advances into a process of *learning* more about students, their needs, their learning styles, and what is needed to grow and make progress through future instruction. The focus is not on teaching but on personalizing the learning process and coaching students to increase proficiency with the targets on the learning progression.

Within a collaborative team, informal formative assessments are not events that teachers plan collaboratively; they are organic moments for teachers to check where learners are in the progression and provide redirection. The collaborative culture comes in with the instructional response. It is essential that when outlining progressions, teams anticipate misconceptions and design corresponding instructional responses. This provides individual teachers with a tool kit of instructional strategies and resources for when they notice that learners may need redirection, whether that comes in the form of reteaching, small-group intervention, or enrichment. Here, there is a marriage of consistency with a shared goal and the autonomy of reacting to the learners and unique needs in each classroom.

Through the scope of the assessment process, informal formative assessment provides another opportunity to answer question 2, How will we know when they have learned it? and opens the door to lean into questions 3 and 4, What will we do when they haven't learned it? and What will we do when they already know it? (DuFour et al., 2016). Once collaborative teams have outlined learning progressions and have reached a common understanding of what proficiency looks like, teachers have the autonomy in the classroom to be instructionally agile and personalize the learning process. To increase confidence and improve instructional strategies, teams may choose to keep a shared document such as the one in figure 4.3 recording common misconceptions and interventions, or simply speak about specific interventions to use in the classroom.

Misconception *If I see this . . .*	Intervention *I can try this . . .*

FIGURE 4.3: Misconception and intervention template.

*Visit **go.SolutionTree.com/assessment** for a free reproducible version of this figure.*

Informal formative assessment puts the focus on accurate and meaningful data (both qualitative and quantitative) that lead to conversations about learning and fostering relationships. It makes each assessment a shared learning experience for teachers and students without any pause in the learning process. Unobtrusive assessment becomes a natural part of classroom instruction, embedded with feedback and continued learning.

Questions for Reflection

*Use these questions to reflect on this chapter's
learning and begin to look forward.*

1. Do we design our learning progressions with intentional alignment to support informal formative assessment and better inform next steps?

2. Do we design our feedback in a way that highlights strengths, redirects the student back to the target, and provides next steps for improvement? How can we improve our feedback methods?

3. How do we ensure that students in our classrooms respond to feedback we provide to them?

4. Does our team or school have a strong understanding of formative assessment as an unobtrusive instructional and learning support that provides a chance for both teachers and students to learn? How is that understanding communicated to students?

5. Do we design our informal classroom assessments with an intentional focus on an instructional response?

6. What informal formative assessment tools have we found to be the most successful for increasing student learning?

Next Steps for Determining Informal Formative Assessments

Understand priority standards and learning progressions to anticipate moments to informally assess.

Use backward design to determine what informal strategies you can use to assess learning and progress.

For each learning target, anticipate misconceptions and possible informal interventions. How will you respond if . . .?

Ensure that each class period is infused with informal assessment to create a student-centered learning experience.

Use observation and informal data to consider the most effective groupings and instructional responses.

chapter five

FORMAL FORMATIVE ASSESSMENT

Assessments are critical to the educational process. Without them, teachers would never know when to move onto the next subject, or how to help students understand concepts better.

—*Andrew Davidson*

Formalized formative assessment, which we often visualize as Formative with a capital *F*, takes on a different form, although the intent parallels that of informal formative assessment. This type of assessment is more obtrusive; that is, it makes it more apparent to students that a check on their learning is taking place. Just like the more unobtrusive type of formative assessment, this more formalized approach should inform choices and decisions moving forward to best meet the needs of each learner.

In this chapter, we address the formal side of formative assessment and its use at the classroom and teacher team levels. In this paradigm, the task types often differ from those of the lowercase-*f* formative assessment of the previous chapter (page 73). And formal formative assessment often involves synchronous, classroom or teamwide administration rather than a more individualized format. This does not always have to be the case, but from a data collection point of view, formal formative assessment is an effective and efficient way to gauge the proficiency of a group of students as a whole and collaborate with teammates. Whether these assessments take place in an individual classroom or in the classrooms of an entire team as common assessments, the intent is to collect data to inform instruction in a penalty-free and supportive environment. When designing and using formal formative assessment, it is important to keep the overall purpose of assessment in mind and remember that learning progressions outline the steps students will take to learn, summative assessment reports whether students have learned it, and formative assessment (whether obtrusive or unobtrusive) informs whether enrichment or intervention is necessary for an individual, a small group, or the whole class.

What Is It?

Formal, capital-*F* formative assessments are strategic checkpoints for teachers and students along the journey of learning. Teachers preplan these points in a unit of study to intentionally check in with students toward the ultimate goal of proficiency with the standards. These more obtrusive formative assessments afford teachers the opportunity to learn about individual students' needs as well as consider future pacing with new skills and content. According to author and educator Rick Wormeli (2018):

> There are many examples of informal formative assessments, such as asking individual questions and assigning spur-of-the-moment journal prompts, but we can't leave formative assessment to chance. Formative assessment must be strategic. We should be able to see specific formative assessments listed in our daily lesson plans. (p. 43)

The use of both informal and formal formative assessment is critical to the learning process. Here, we will explore how these formal assessments function as pauses during instruction as well as their planning, development, and use.

A Time to Pause

While informal formative assessment addresses the moments throughout a class period or school day when teachers take in live information in order to make on-the-spot decisions, formal formative assessment is a time to pause. This type of assessment does not have to be long, but it differs in implementation from the fluid informal formative assessment and feedback routines that dominate the daily classroom experience. Formal formative assessments should not happen every day, as this causes a classroom to feel assessment heavy and instructionally light. Too much obtrusive formative assessment makes teaching seem like a start-and-stop enterprise, and it can make scoring and data collection cumbersome for teachers. It can cause students to constantly feel judged.

Formal formative assessment is, however, undoubtedly an integral part of the learning process; think of it like a water break on a long hike, when the hikers can check their map and gauge how things are going. The little corrections along the way, like stepping over tree roots and moving low branches out of the way, are informal formative assessments, and the hikers reserve summative judgment until the end of the hike.

The Planning of Formal Formative Assessment

The two types of formative assessment differ in when teachers craft them. Although not an absolute difference, teachers usually plan and create the more formal, obtrusive formative assessment tools in advance of a unit of study, while they do not necessarily create informal formative assessment tools ahead of time. Teachers would not and could not preplan an on-the-spot formative assessment such as a quick conversation. This type of assessment naturally happens throughout the course of instruction and practice. But for explicit formative assessment, teachers anticipate the moments when a formalized check-in would be appropriate and plan accordingly.

Imagine a middle school French class will be working on a unit of study that involves the skill of interpreting spoken language. In essence, the students will have to listen in the target language (French) and understand the spoken word. For this particular unit, the theme is traveling in a French-speaking country or region. With the ultimate goal of interpreting language, students will need to practice listening to vocabulary and grammatical constructions they encounter in order to make sense of what people are saying. They will need to practice making inferences from context to support comprehension. As a formal formative assessment, the teacher could provide students with recordings that they will have to interpret with a written or verbal response. The teacher might do this one or more times during the unit with increasing complexity until the students are at a level that the teacher considers proficient and show that they are prepared for summative assessment. The teacher would plan these check-ins prior to the unit and then use them along with more informal formative assessment to gauge student progress and respond.

The Development of Formal Formative Assessment Tools

Learning progressions are the starting place for creating formative assessment tools for formal use. Since the learning targets are the skills teachers have identified as stepping-stones to proficiency, it is natural for teachers to develop tools that will gauge student progress aligned to these targets. However, teachers need not assess every learning target in a progression through formal formative assessment; there will be some that they only address informally. In order to determine which targets to include in formal formative assessment, teachers should consider which targets are difficult for students to learn and challenging for teachers to teach. This lens provides teachers with direction when narrowing down a list of learning targets to assess in a formal manner. If this type of assessment is to serve its purpose of informing next steps, the information and evidence of learning that teachers gather must be of a manageable amount.

Teachers should determine the appropriate format of a formal formative assessment following the same guidance as for summative assessment. They should let the target be the guide for how to best elicit evidence of learning. Teachers can use selected-response, constructed-response, or performance-based assessments, but selected and constructed responses may be best suited for this purpose. Selected- and constructed-response items allow for quick data collection, leading to efficient analysis and response. Performance-based assessments are usually longer and require the use of a rubric for scoring, so the final product lends itself to summative purposes. A shorter performance-based assessment or a preliminary draft of a larger summative assessment may be appropriate for an obtrusive formative assessment; it simply depends on the learning target and the skill that students must demonstrate.

In the following sections, we present examples of tasks that teachers can use formally and how they would employ them in the classroom. To make these events formal in nature, teachers must intentionally plan how they will infuse the formative assessments into the class flow, what role the assessments will have in the delivery of feedback, and how they will use evidence from the assessment process for further coaching. While some of the ideas and tools we present may not be new, the focus that we are placing on their formal, obtrusive use and the instructional response that follows may be. The level of student understanding that teachers observe and the data that they gather allow each *F*ormative assessment to be a learning experience for all.

Socratic Seminars

While teachers can use Socratic seminars in the summative domain, we will focus here on their formative use. Through Socratic discussions, teachers expect students to lead and maintain the discussion on a given series of questions or prompts. There are many ways to facilitate a Socratic discussion, and one way might be more effective than another depending on the context. In order for the seminar to be considered formative, teachers must maintain focus on the instructional response to the data collected through student discussion.

To conduct a Socratic seminar, the teacher poses a question or series of questions about a text or topic after students have read or learned about it. While teachers can do this on the spot, many let students know of the assessment in advance so they can prepare their thoughts and ideas. During a Socratic discussion, the teacher takes a secondary role as students, often sitting in a circle (or inner and outer circles), respond to one another, comment on one another's comments, and even ask their own questions to keep the conversation going. To ensure that all students are contributing, teachers may choose to give students cards representing questions and comments (for example, each student gets two comment cards and one question card for the discussion). Students receive a set number of these blank cards to ensure that speaking opportunities are balanced. When students are ready to contribute to the discussion, they make a comment or ask a question and then return the appropriate card to the teacher.

No matter how the Socratic seminar occurs, teachers can take notes on student thoughts, ideas, and questions to prepare to respond to the activity during the following day's class period. Tools such as figure 5.1 allow teachers to record student responses and questions throughout the seminar on the prepared prompts. Teachers can jot students' names down with their thoughts or needs in each box.

Prompts	Comments and Responses	Questions
What changes would you have made to _____?		
Why do you think the author made the decision to _____?		
Can you propose an alternative solution to _____?		

FIGURE 5.1: Socratic seminar template.

*Visit **go.SolutionTree.com/assessment** for a free reproducible version of this figure.*

Graphic Organizers

Graphic organizers give students a formative opportunity to brainstorm and in turn gather, organize, and categorize their thoughts on a given topic. Teachers commonly use these organizers at all grade levels. Feedback from teachers is critical for students to produce high-quality work. That is, the formal formative use of organizers paired with feedback leads students toward a successful summative product.

Graphic organizers take numerous forms, from Venn diagrams, which allow students to highlight differences and similarities between concepts, to T-charts, which allow students to identify terms and definitions or claims and the evidence tied to them. Frayer diagrams are useful to define and characterize concepts, and idea webs are helpful to show how ideas all relate to a central topic. The list goes on, and a quick online search can yield a plethora of options to use in various contexts. The focus here is not on the various graphic organizer formats but rather on how teachers can use graphic organizers to support learning and growth.

Teachers monitor students' use of graphic organizers by observation, and they assess and give feedback either while observing students working on the organizers or after collecting them. Students can then make revisions and expand their thinking. Graphic organizers are valuable, obtrusive formative checks throughout a learning progression that can ask students to, among other things, support claims, compare and contrast ideas, define terms, or cite evidence. For some students, a visual representation of their thinking is a beneficial way to increase their knowledge and skills. No matter whether teachers use a digital or hard-copy version, they must select an organizer that will lend itself to further student learning and the demonstration of that learning.

Drafting of Projects and Writing Assignments

When students complete longer writing assignments and projects, they follow clear steps to produce the final product. Teachers usually assess the end product summatively, but the process leading up to it is formative. By allowing early drafts of a writing assignment or project to be formal formative assessments, teachers build in checks along the way to the final iteration. These checks are important for teachers to ensure that the students are progressing with their learning and understanding what the final product should look or sound like. These formative markers also help scaffold the work for students and provide pacing for these long-term assessments. Students can concurrently see their academic progress as well as work on their time-management skills.

A feedback loop (Sadler, 1989) is an essential part of any drafting process. Students produce evidence, teachers provide feedback, students act on that feedback, and the cycle continues. There is also power in incorporating peer feedback and self-assessment into the drafting process. This is a different implementation of a feedback loop but uses the same processes.

Quizzing

Quizzes to gauge student proficiency are very common, as well as very informative when teachers use them well. The length of a quiz should be relatively short—only as many questions as the teacher needs to gauge where students are with their learning. Questions must respect the complexity of the target they are assessing, and teachers must write them so that they and students can interpret the results in order to improve. While quizzes are a more traditional form of formal formative assessment, it is essential to remember the intent of these experiences is not scoring but using evidence to inform instruction and learning. Teachers must ensure that they tightly align quizzes to learning targets and that they use quizzes for the purpose of facilitating a targeted instructional response.

Digital platforms are extremely useful for developing quizzes, especially for less complex learning targets. A wide variety of these tools can quickly gauge whether students are able to identify, recall, or recognize simple ideas or concepts. For this purpose, many times quiz questions appear in a selected-response format, and the score is automatically generated for the teacher and student. Digital tools can also be useful for more complex targets, but with questions that yield a constructed response, the teacher will need to look at the individual pieces of evidence in order to give feedback to students, rather than using automated scoring.

Some digital platforms embed formative quizzing within content delivery rather than after instruction has occurred. For example, students may read and interpret content on slides and then answer a comprehension question before moving on to another few slides. The teacher can get live information on student results and can then take immediate corrective action if necessary. These types of activities can be teacher paced or student paced. Sometimes, teachers may find it is more productive to do an activity like this as a class, waiting for all students to respond to an obtrusive formative question before moving on, and other times, it would be more appropriate for students to move at their own pace.

As an example, consider a middle school computer science class that is using the digital quizzing tool Kahoot! (https://kahoot.com) to do a quick check on vocabulary acquisition. The teacher has set the norm that as she moves through the questions, she will pause the digital quiz to reteach and review if, as a class, students score below 80 percent on any question. After the quiz is complete, the teacher reviews the whole-class data to look student by student for anyone who may need individual support.

Group Work

Many students find collaboration an effective way to learn. In the formative realm, students can work together to create or complete a preplanned instructional activity. They can express their ideas, thoughts, and understandings all while listening to others and expanding their thinking: "Students' interactions and discussions with others allow the group to construct new knowledge, place it within a conceptual framework of existing knowledge, and then refine and assess what they know and do not know" (Washington University in St. Louis, n.d.). Working as a group can be a vulnerable process, so relying on sound relationships and trust can make it easier for students to feel comfortable sharing. Establishing norms for group work early in the school year creates a safe and structured environment. Group work is a great way for students to explore a topic without direct guidance from the teacher. Once their teacher has provided the objective, students can set out on the journey of learning together and use the teacher as a resource when necessary.

Through group work, teachers gather evidence of learning as well as information on how students work together. Teachers can provide feedback on all aspects of student academic performance and behavioral skills. They might use a checklist when walking around and observing small groups and their work. Figure 5.2 provides an example of a checklist to use to gather formative evidence while students are working in small groups. This figure represents an elementary science classroom working on data collection with how the same plant grows in different environments. As the teacher walks around, she specifically observes each student's data collection table, how they present that data in a graph, as well as their attention to the work. In addition to on-the-spot coaching, she also jots notes of observed needs for further follow-up at the individual level.

Student Name	Learning Target 1: Gather data in a table.	Learning Target 2: Present data in a graph.	On-Task Behavior
Violet	☑ Proficient ☐ Improving ☐ No evidence	☑ Proficient ☐ Improving ☐ No evidence	☐ Consistent ☑ Sometimes ☐ Seldom
Orion	☑ Proficient ☐ Improving ☐ No evidence	☐ Proficient ☑ Improving *Review parts of graph.* ☐ No evidence	☑ Consistent ☐ Sometimes ☐ Seldom
Shreeya	☐ Proficient ☑ Improving *Unorganized data, which led to no graph yet. Follow up.* ☐ No evidence	☐ Proficient ☐ Improving ☑ No evidence	☑ Consistent ☐ Sometimes ☐ Seldom

FIGURE 5.2: Student group work observation template.

*Visit **go.SolutionTree.com/assessment** for a free reproducible version of this figure.*

Jigsaw

The jigsaw method was first developed in the 1970s by Elliot Aronson (1978). It has since been widely researched and adapted. Teachers can use this method of formal formative assessment to support students with summarization skills that cross over into multiple content areas. Jigsaw activities come in various formats—what follows is one example.

In this example, the teacher breaks a longer reading into several smaller chunks and has different student groups read each one. The students then break into different groups, containing a student from each of the original reading groups, and share what they have read and learned. Teachers can have students document their work, they can meet with the individual groups, or they can have a whole-class discussion to assess and ensure understanding. In order to gather formative data to use for an instructional response, teachers must be cautious with a jigsaw activity and ensure that all students are actively engaged and work together to create a shared understanding of the entire piece of reading. Providing a straightforward process for the jigsaw and carefully monitoring students makes for a successful experience. Teachers must be mindful about which reading selections would be a good fit (both with content and text complexity) for this type of formative assessment. The level of complexity must be accessible to all students in order to be appropriate.

No matter which method of formal formative assessment teachers use, it should maximize the opportunities for students and teachers to gauge proficiency and determine next steps. Assessment is a catalyst for learning when students know a checkpoint exists to support their success moving forward. The design of these checkpoints is crucial; as Erkens (2019) writes, "A team's ability to increase student achievement levels depends on how well it designs the assessments named within its road maps in advance of providing the instruction" (p. 74). Figure 5.3 (page 100) is a planning form for creating a high-quality formative assessment tool from *The Big Book of Tools for Collaborative Teams in a PLC at Work®* by William M. Ferriter (2020). This tool is crafted for a team-created assessment, but individuals can also use it. It highlights not only the assessment method but also the complexity of the target and anticipated errors or mistakes that may occur.

The Use of Formal Formative Assessment

When administering formative assessment in the formal realm, teachers must make sure students know it is a time to show what they can do in a low-risk environment. While the purpose of both types of formative assessment is determining an instructional response based on student need, some schools or teams require the scoring of formal formative events. Even in this situation, teachers should not use

Essential Learning Target to Be Assessed:

Depth of Knowledge of the Target	Best Strategy for Assessing This Target	Percentage of Questions on District Benchmarks and Standardized Tests That Cover This Target	How Important This Target Is for Future Success in and Beyond School
☐ Recall and Reproduction ☐ Skills and Concepts ☐ Strategic Thinking ☐ Extended Thinking	☐ Selected response ☐ Constructed response ☐ Performance based ☐ Other _____	☐ 0–5 percent ☐ 6–10 percent ☐ 11–15 percent ☐ More than 15 percent	☐ Not important ☐ Somewhat important ☐ Very important ☐ Essential

Potential Assessment Questions

Question	Expected Answer	Common Mistakes We Might See

Source: Adapted from Ferriter, 2020.

FIGURE 5.3: Planning tool for formal formative assessment.

Visit go.SolutionTree.com/assessment for a free reproducible version of this figure.

these scores in a summative way (for grading) when assessing learning targets. Instead, they can use them to help students prepare for the eventual summative assessment. For this to happen, teachers must explain to students what their score means with regard to proficiency. It is important to provide formal formative assessment, as students will continue to learn more about what their final product or skill will look like at the end of the unit.

Again, formal formative assessment tools do not have to be long; the length of the assessment should be determined by the amount of evidence the teacher needs to make decisions moving forward. This may mean that the assessment is three questions or seven questions. It may mean that students are writing a sentence or a paragraph. What matters is that teachers are able to determine whether they can elicit accurate inferences of student understanding from the assessment tool paired with evidence from the students.

For example, consider a third-grade class doing a geometry unit in which the students are studying perimeter and area. The teacher is planning to give students an exit ticket, formatively assessing their understanding. In this case, eight to ten questions are not necessary. The teacher designs two questions that prompt students to find the area and perimeter, as well as clearly show their work, which allows her to assess the target and gather sufficient information to determine next steps. In contrast, think of a high school Spanish class where students are learning how to use direct object pronouns in sentences. The teacher would need several questions (possibly five to seven) in order to determine student proficiency. He would want to see if the students could demonstrate the skill with consistency.

If teachers feel that they are getting inaccurate information from formal formative assessment based on the evidence they are seeing in day-to-day informal assessment, they should investigate the situation. A strong relationship between student and teacher can allow for productive conversations about inconsistencies because trust has formed. Through this trust, the teacher can clearly explain the purpose of the assessment, figure out why the student's results do not align with daily classroom happenings, and move forward together. This is how teachers bridge learning with formative assessment and remind students that it is all part of a larger process.

For example, a teacher receives a low-quality, partially incomplete formative assessment from a student. This student has previously shown proficiency during her lowercase-*f* formative work and assessment. After a conversation with the student, the teacher realizes that the student does not want to complete the current assessment because she does not feel like it counts. This is a common problem when students have been trained to think that in order for something to be of value, it must be worth points or contribute to their grade. For assessment to truly contribute to learning, teachers must undo this mindset and teach students to value feedback and continued learning over arbitrary scores while still in the process of learning. Teachers must clearly show students that the purpose of these check-ins on student learning is to inform future learning and instruction. In essence, formative assessment "counts" toward a final grade because it is readying students for summative assessment, not because a score is going in the gradebook. The formative process should allow for mistakes in a low-risk environment in order to build confidence for summative assessment.

Among the other considerations that teachers should keep in mind when using formal formative assessments are timing the assessments, scoring them (only if necessary), reducing students' assessment anxiety, and employing data notebooks to help students track their own progress.

Timing Assessments

The timing of formal formative assessments should be planned out prior to the beginning of the unit with a strong alignment to the learning progression. That is, teachers must decide not only which learning targets will warrant obtrusive formative assessment but also when those will fall within the unit of study. Figure 5.4 is an example of a learning progression, the type of formative assessment (informal or formal) this teacher would use for each target, and what tool the teacher would use for assessment.

Standard: Develop a model that illustrates the relationship between the Earth, moon, and sun. (adapted from MS-ESS1-1)		
Learning Progression (Targets)	Formative Assessment Type	Assessment Tool
I can recognize scientific vocabulary.	Informal	Daily classroom practice identifying scientific vocabulary in text and determining its meaning
I can define scientific vocabulary.	Informal, formal	Classroom assignments—journaling and small-group work Quiz
I can research various technologies.	Informal	Guided practice with the teacher, conferencing, and collaborative work

I can evaluate how technology is used to study the universe.	Informal	Classroom practice through discussion
I can explain the relationship between the Earth, moon, and sun.	Formal	Quick write

Source for modified standard: NGSS Lead States, 2013.

FIGURE 5.4: Assessment alignment template.

*Visit **go.SolutionTree.com/assessment** for a free reproducible version of this figure.*

The preceding template serves as an example that teachers can use to assess targets in a multitude of ways and at different moments in time. What is important is that the teacher plans this beforehand and knows which targets will be the focus for a formal formative assessment tool. Teachers can also determine how they will collect the evidence from the formal tool and how they will disseminate the feedback to move learners forward. Remember, not every formative experience will be preplanned. The figure represents ideas that the teacher could easily add to or change. Teachers can simplify this template by not filling out the particular assessment tools for the targets that they will address informally (only including those they will assess formally) and leaving those to lesson planning and the natural progression of the classroom.

Scoring Assessments (If Necessary)

Scoring a formative assessment tool may seem to be an oxymoron. Since teachers use the data to inform themselves and students about the path forward rather than to judge proficiency, a score is not necessary. It is possible to score formative assessments; however, since they occur during the learning process, teachers should not use these results for a final determination of proficiency. In fact, teachers should only score formal formative assessments if the score has a clear purpose (quantitative data tracking). Obtrusive formative assessment experiences are more formalized and can have a similar feel or format to a summative assessment, but they must not become one and the same. If teachers use formative assessment to make a final judgment about proficiency and it impacts a grade, the assessment is no longer formative. That is a purpose of summative assessment.

If teachers do score a formative assessment, they can pair it with feedback in order to ensure that students know where they are as well as where they are headed.

Students must also know that they are still in the process of learning with formative assessment—a good result means they are on track to become proficient. Lower results are not a sentence of failure; rather, they are a moment to recalibrate and determine where misconceptions lie and what is necessary to move forward. Since scoring on the formal side of the formative realm may miscommunicate overall proficiency, as these tools are assessing targets and not standards, teachers must be mindful in how they communicate results. They must direct students to focus on feedback over scores because learning is ongoing. Students must view this score as a checkpoint and not an end point. In the end, whether or not teachers score formative assessment, summative evidence of proficiency with the standards should determine the final grade.

Reducing Assessment Anxiety

Formal formative assessment has many uses in the academic realm, but it can also serve the emotional needs of some students by reducing assessment anxiety. Since the experience is more formal, this type of obtrusive formative assessment can help students prepare for the summative process and build their confidence through the incorporation of coaching and feedback. The summative process should be transparent from the outset of a unit, and students should gain experience with what they will need to do through intentional and supportive formative design. If students get very nervous before tests but have several opportunities through formal formative assessment to answer similar types of questions, receive feedback, and develop their skills, their confidence should grow moving into the summative assessment. As Rick Stiggins (1999) states, "Students succeed academically only if they want to succeed and feel capable of doing so" (p. 192). The key is that students should not feel that summative assessment is a gotcha moment. Teachers can achieve this environment through a robust formative process and practice with formal formative assessment tools.

Employing Data Notebooks

With formal formative assessment, student investment plays a significant role. As Steve Chappuis, Carol Commodore, and Rick Stiggins (2017) write, teachers must "conduct assessment activities that directly involve students, engage them in setting goals for what comes next in their learning, and teach them to track their progress toward that goal" (p. 6). One way for students to monitor their own proficiency and progress and therefore invest in their learning is with digital or paper data notebooks. These notebooks should house data from obtrusive formative assessments to show performance and growth over time with the standards and targets, and they can also keep summative assessment information to capture final proficiency levels. Data may come in the form of numbers or letters if the assessment is scored, but there are many other ways to represent data, such as short descriptions or color-coded targets that indicate what students have learned. No matter how they represent the data, students must understand the meaning of the symbols or indicators of proficiency. They must also achieve balance in the amount of data—not too much and not too little. Teachers will guide which data will go in the notebook and how they should represent the data. The data collection cannot become a cumbersome task that takes away from the learning experience. These notebooks should be supporting tools that show where students are and how they have grown in order to determine next steps.

The data from formal formative assessments (and summative assessments) should be kept by standard or target, not by task type. It is much more informative to see results organized by skill to get a clear picture of student proficiency. Otherwise, students could have to look in more than one place to find out how they are doing with an individual skill. If multiple assessments address one particular standard or target and they are scored and reported simply by the task type, such as *test*, students (and teachers) will have to look in a few different places to find evidence on that target or standard. This can make it more difficult for students to focus on developing skills rather than just doing well on a given task.

Data notebooks serve as a tool to support self-advocacy for students. For example, if a teacher asks students to analyze their performance on a formal formative assessment, they can interpret the results and determine whether they need enrichment or additional support with a skill. Figure 5.5 (page 106) provides a summary tool for student data notebooks. This tool helps students track their proficiency with two learning targets on three different dates in a unit of study. Notice there is no place to put the task type. It could be added if desired, but the focus is on the skill and whether the student is achieving proficiency rather than finding success on a particular task.

Learning for Teachers

The way teachers learn through the formal formative assessment process cannot be completely separated from the other assessment processes since its connection to informal formative assessment and summative assessment is critical. The day-in, day-out assessment of students works hand in hand with what teachers determine important to assess formally. Formal formative assessment also gives teachers confidence when moving to summative assessment. Once students have shown proficiency through more obtrusive formative assessment, teachers are prepared to use the summative process to confirm student understanding and skill development.

Student name: *Aleeya M.*

Date: *October 23*

Standard: Describe the roles of political, civil, and economic organizations in shaping people's lives. (D2.Civ.6.6-8)

Learning Targets	I've got it!	I'm still working on it.	I need to get started.	Evidence
Target 1: Define political, civil, and economic organizations.		X		*I have looked up these terms but have not taken the definitions and made them my own.*
Target 2: Explain the roles of political, civil, and economic organizations.			X	

Date: *October 30*

Learning Targets	I've got it!	I'm still working on it.	I need to get started.	Evidence
Target 1: Define political, civil, and economic organizations.		X		*I am still working on defining these terms for myself but am almost done.*

Learning Targets	I've got it!	I'm still working on it.	I need to get started.	Evidence
Date: *November 3*				
Target 2: Explain the roles of political, civil, and economic organizations.		X		*I started writing my explanation of the roles of these organizations.*
Target 1: Define political, civil, and economic organizations.	X			*I completed the chart with the short with the dictionary definitions and my definitions of the terms. I received feedback from the teacher and revised.*
Target 2: Explain the roles of political, civil, and economic organizations.		X		*I used my definitions of the terms to explain the role of each one. I worked with a peer to assess and revise my work.*

FIGURE 5.5: Data notebook summary tool.

Source for standard: National Council for the Social Studies, 2017.

Visit go.SolutionTree.com/assessment for a free reproducible version of this figure.

Through formal formative assessment, teachers also learn about the different ways to assess learning targets to ensure efficiency and effectiveness. This is never a perfect process. Teachers may develop a formative assessment tool that they believe will generate good information but, after using the tool, may realize that it has some inadequacies. This is the moment when teachers want to find out more about their assessment methods rather than after the summative assessment. Recreating a summative assessment tool because of invalid evidence is much more difficult than revising assessments on the formative side.

As previously mentioned, a formal formative assessment tool can have a selected-response format, which makes compiling data easy for teachers. However, if teachers use a constructed-response assessment tool, they will need to determine what they will accept as evidence of proficiency before they administer the assessment, and they will need to make sure that this is clear to the students. Teachers learn through the process of considering what it would take to show proficiency with the targets and a readiness to move forward.

Learning for Students

Students learn about their proficiency, where their proficiency lies on the learning progression, and what evidence of learning is acceptable for each target through the formal formative assessment process. In this way, students become partners in the assessment journey. Teachers share examples and descriptions of what high-quality work looks and sounds like, and as students learn more, their confidence grows. Formal formative assessment gives students an opportunity to practice showing what they know and can do. It is the middle ground between the very informal, day-to-day assessment–feedback loop and the summative assessment process.

Students also continue to gain knowledge about what particular standards ask them to demonstrate. When teachers assess using a more formalized tool, students can clearly see the expectations required to prove proficiency. When students are clear on what they need to do, they are more successful. If the goal changes or is unknown, students are taking a shot in the dark on how to best prepare and, in turn, how to perform.

Having students track their progress is an effective way to maximize student investment. Students learn about their growth and readiness when they regularly access their data and see what progress they are making based on their results. The effective use of data notebooks, as discussed previously, helps increase students' investment in their learning, which in turn contributes to success in the future.

When teachers work together as teams, they can shed light on where students are and work together to support them through formal formative assessment.

Collaboration Around Assessment

All types of formative assessment, both formal and informal, are used to determine next steps in learning for students. In the formal formative realm, it is essential for teachers to collaboratively determine what skills they will assess from their learning progressions and how they will assess them. The collaboration continues with the analysis of results and the decisions that they make for individual students as well as classes and grade levels as a whole.

Teachers can work together on the topics of summative and formative assessment, but with formal formative assessment, collaboration plays the most critical role. With obtrusive formative assessment, question 2 (How will we know when they have learned it?) gets answered to clearly move into discussions about scaffolding and enrichment (questions 3 and 4: What will we do when they haven't learned it? and What will we do when they already know it?; DuFour et al., 2016).

A frequent use of formal formative assessment is common assessment. Teachers create, administer, and analyze these assessment tools as a collaborative team, especially in schools or districts that function as PLCs. According to Cassandra Erkens (2016):

> A collaborative common assessment is any assessment, formative or summative, that is either team created or team endorsed in advance of instruction and then administered in close proximity by all instructors so they can collaboratively examine the results, plan instructionally agile responses, analyze errors, and explore areas for program improvement. (p. 7)

The power of common assessment lies in the ability of a team of teachers to work together to create assessment tools, determine success criteria, and plan intervention and enrichment stemming from the same assessment event. Teacher teams should keep in mind that common formative assessments serve four primary purposes (DuFour & DuFour, 2012).

1. To help teachers identify students who are struggling to master—or who are already proficient with—essential concepts and skills

2. To help students track their own progress toward mastering essential concepts and skills

3.   To provide teachers with evidence of their *individual* pedagogical strengths and weaknesses

4.   To provide teams with evidence of their *collective* pedagogical strengths and weaknesses

Teacher teams must ensure tight alignment to their targets by determining which targets they will use for common assessment. Teams do not need to commonly assess all targets. Rather, teachers can collaborate and select those targets that will facilitate robust conversations and planning for student learning. Which are difficult for students to learn and challenging for teachers to teach? If teachers select targets for common assessment that are relatively easy for students, the follow-up data meeting will not be as useful or productive as it could be. It is worth celebrating if everyone finds success, but this may also mean that the teachers did not tackle some of the most difficult parts of teaching as a collaborative team.

If, for example, a team of fourth-grade teachers choose to assess a target from a progression that simply has students identify the definitions of vocabulary words, it is not that the assessment is invalid. The assessment will work as it should if the intended outcome is to see whether students can match terms with definitions for the purpose of using them in class moving forward. However, selecting this target for a common assessment may not be as useful as something more complex. Teachers will gather the data and have a quick conversation about which words students missed, but they will not engage in a deep discussion about how students are demonstrating a transferable skill or which teaching practices are best supporting student learning.

It is wise to consider a more complex skill such as using context clues to determine the meaning of words. When teachers get together after a common formative assessment on this skill, the conversations about how best to support students with scaffolding and enrichment as well as the sharing of teaching strategies will be very valuable. Determining meaning from context is a skill that students will use at every grade level. It can be very difficult for some students, and teachers will need to have a valid and reliable way to gauge proficiency and determine next steps as a team. A conversation about a skill that is difficult for students rather than something simple ensures that teams are maximizing their time.

Another consideration to ensure learning for collaborative teams is to limit the number of targets per common assessment. They must collect data for each target, and if there are too many, it takes much longer to aggregate the information in order to analyze it. Two to three targets for a common formative assessment is doable from both a student and teacher standpoint. Then, the assessment does not have to be long, and the meeting to analyze data and plan next steps can happen in a timely fashion.

Figure 5.6 is an example of a learning progression that identifies not only the informal and formal formative assessments but also the common formative assessments (which are also formal). This is just one example of how to effectively map out both types of formative assessments. Once teachers determine how they will go about assessment throughout a unit of study, this assessment framework offers guidance for a path to proficiency for students, and a guideline for collaborative team discussions on assessment, intervention, and enrichment.

Standard: Determine two or more central ideas of a text and analyze their development over the course of the text, including how they interact and build on one another to provide a complex analysis; provide an objective summary of the text. (RI.11-12.2)		
Learning Progression (Targets)	Formative Assessment Type	Assessment Tool
I can find multiple central ideas of an informational text.	Informal	Class discussion
I can explain the development of the central ideas throughout an informational text.	Informal, common formal	Guided practice, constructed-response quiz
I can analyze the development of the central ideas throughout an informational text (how they interact and build on one another).	Formal	Socratic seminar
I can provide an objective summary of an informational text.	Formal	Written summary of a given text

Source for standard: NGA & CCSSO, 2010a.

FIGURE 5.6: Sample learning progression assessment alignment.

*Visit **go.SolutionTree.com/assessment** for a free reproducible version of this figure.*

For singleton teachers—that is, teachers who are the only ones who teach a particular grade level or course at their school—a common assessment may be somewhat different. Some schools, instead of developing a common assessment for each grade level or course, choose a skill that crosses content areas and grade levels. For example, a smaller school may have only one teacher at each elementary grade level. Rather than having a common assessment for a specific grade-level reading standard, the teachers may choose a skill that appears in multiple grade levels, such as determining the main idea or theme of a text. Each grade level would have an assessment on that skill at an appropriate level of complexity. Then teachers could collaboratively talk about proficiency at the different levels and next steps for all students. This vertical articulation supports tight alignment in selecting priority standards for various grade levels as well as in establishing what teachers expect each year.

Questions for
Reflection

*Use these questions to reflect on this chapter's
learning and begin to look forward.*

1. Have we determined which targets from the learning
    progression we should assess formally?

2. Do we design our formal formative assessment tools prior to
    the outset of the unit to ensure alignment and student growth?

3. Do our formal formative assessments provide valid evidence of
    learning aligned to the learning progression?

4. Do we set aside time for our collaborative team to analyze
    formal formative assessment results?

5. Do we have structures in place for our students who need
    additional support or enrichment?

6. How do our students take an active role in collecting data from
    their formal formative assessments?

Next Steps for Determining Formal Formative Assessments

Analyze current common and individual processes of formal formative assessment for effectiveness and efficiency.

Revise assessment tools as necessary to ensure alignment with the selected essential learning targets.

Create new assessment tools as necessary for any essential learning targets that have not been addressed by formal formative assessment in the past.

When appropriate, create or revise scoring guides to support accurate interpretation of results for students and teachers.

Ensure time is set aside during collaborative team meetings to analyze data.

Take action according to the assessment results for additional support and enrichment.

chapter six

DAILY INSTRUCTION:
Assessment Comes Full Circle

*Our great mistake in education is, as it seems to me, the worship
of book-learning—the confusion of instruction and education.
We strain the memory instead of cultivating the mind.*

—John Lubbock

The assessment process comes full circle with instruction, the focus of this chapter. Day-to-day interactions in the classroom are critical when considering the assessment process as a learning experience. Instruction takes on so many different forms, yet no matter the method teachers use, they can gather evidence of student learning, student engagement, and teacher efficacy.

It is easier to make decisions about how best to spend class time when everyone sees current practices as a process by which to make future plans not only for students but also for teachers. This intentionality with instruction forms and strengthens relationships while providing targeted support for students. Teachers can always map out standards and content ahead of time, but being agile with instructional planning from day to day ensures that they are meeting student needs. This is where teacher teams can strike the balance between consistency and autonomy—that is, maintaining consistency with their standards, progressions, and expectations, while autonomously bringing them to life for students.

What Is It?

Writing about instruction without relying heavily on the assessment process would be nearly impossible. This is the reason instruction comes last in this book, as it brings the assessment cycle full circle. Teachers cannot make instruction purposeful without first understanding intended learning outcomes and aligning assessment, and subsequently instruction, to learning progressions. It is the marriage of alignment to these progressions with an allowance for instructional agility that makes instruction impactful, purposeful, and student centered.

While learning progressions outline the pace and structure of a unit for instructional purposes, as well as the formative and summative assessment plan, the decisions that teachers make on a daily basis must center on students' emerging needs. Thus, when planning instruction, teachers should carefully consider the infusion of assessment. Teachers can reflect on the question: *How will I know if students have learned it?* Assessment should be an integral part of every lesson taught. It would be ideal for students to always learn whatever teachers teach when they teach it, but that is far from the reality of the typical classroom, and teachers must go about instruction with the mindset and understanding that they will pivot based on emerging evidence. Whether it comes to learning the scientific method, crafting a quality essay, dribbling a soccer ball, or perfecting the ability to add and subtract fractions, students enter the classroom with different prerequisite knowledge and needs. Teachers can address this diversity among students through carefully pairing assessment and daily instruction.

Pairing Instruction and Assessment

Instruction is not simply the process of delivering content; rather, it's a teacher-student partnership to ensure that learning occurs. At the end of every class period or school day, a teacher should be able to answer the question, I've taught it, but what evidence do I have that they have learned it? Planning instruction involves pondering that question and embedding assessment and discussion into new learning. There are many ways to do this, which we highlight in the following sections: guided instruction, questioning, collaborative learning, and strategic grouping.

Guided Instruction

There is a tremendous difference between teaching and learning. All instructors have had moments in which they taught a topic, and students just didn't learn as well as they planned. Embedding assessment into daily instruction is necessary so teachers can catch those moments and make on-the-spot decisions and adjustments. Without this attention to assessment, students could be left behind, disengage, or lose hope and efficacy in the learning process. Douglas Fisher and Nancy Frey (2010) introduce the idea of *guided instruction* as "saying or doing the just-right thing to get the learner to do cognitive work" (p. vii). Instruction is more than just teaching the content and skills; it needs to involve learners in the delivery and consumption of material. Guided instruction is not a classroom routine but a set of teacher behaviors that ensure student learning. Fisher and Frey (2010) outline the teacher behaviors and instructional practices that make up quality guided instruction as follows.

- *Questioning* to check for student understanding

- *Prompts* "to facilitate students' cognitive and metacognitive processes and processing" (Fisher & Frey, 2010, p. xvi)

- *Cues* to draw students' attention to key information or common errors

- *Explanations* and *modeling* to support students when they "do not have sufficient knowledge to complete tasks" (Fisher & Frey, 2010, p. xvi)

Guided instruction personalizes the learning process to ensure that students are doing the brunt of the work while the teacher is making intentional instructional decisions. These decisions are designed to provide support through questioning, prompts, cues, and explanations and modeling to promote increased learning and results.

Questioning

Questioning is one of the key elements of effective formative assessment (Black, Harrison, Lee, Marshall, & Wiliam, 2003). Research on questioning in the class-room is in broad strokes; it does not contain a definitive conclusion as to what types of questions or which questioning strategies yield the most positive results. While a certain question type might not prove to be more effective (especially when considering grade levels and content areas), teachers can carefully craft questions that maximize the information they are able to receive and act upon. Fisher and Frey (2009b) suggest that questions asked of students should feed forward to allow for targeted and modified future instruction.

A core reaction from the teacher when a student answers a question is to judge the correctness of the response. However, in order to explore and use instructional agility and to infuse assessment into daily instruction, it is necessary that teachers ask higher-level cognitive questions because these questions lead to greater inferences about student understanding.

Lower-level cognitive questions are those that ask students to merely recall information. These are normally closed questions, or ones that do not promote increased dialogue. Through lower-level cognitive questions, promptly deciding correct versus incorrect answers is fairly easy, but understanding student thinking and finding the evidence necessary to adjust instruction or provide feedback proves rather challenging. The teacher's response to lower-level cognitive questions requires a rapid analysis and inference of what is happening in students' minds.

On the other hand, higher-level cognitive questions are those that ask students to not only provide an answer but also manipulate and synthesize information in order to support their position with logical reasoning. These open-ended questions allow for conversation and a deeper dive into understanding what the learner knows or does not know. They offer the teacher a chance to respond appropriately, whether that be through a follow-up question or feedback. Higher-level cognitive questions look beyond right or wrong and grant the teacher the ability to have a more in-depth understanding of students' thought processes. Figure 6.1 provides examples of open and closed questions.

Closed Questions	Open Questions
What answer did you get for number five?	How did you arrive at your answer for number five?
When did that occur?	How did the series of events leading up to that date effect the outcome?
Does that make sense?	What about that process confuses you?
Do you have any questions?	What questions do you have?
Did you use evidence from the text to support your conclusion?	What events in the story led you to that conclusion?
Do you agree with my answer?	What advice would you give me to improve my answer? How would that help me improve?

FIGURE 6.1: Open and closed questions.

Collaborative Learning

Collaborative learning is the partnership of students, or students and teachers, to engage in the process of learning together. It removes the teacher as the primary owner of the knowledge and makes the learning process a joint effort. To help explain how to make instruction and learning more cooperative, imagine that a physical education teacher is working with students on how to serve a volleyball underhand. Instead of modeling the correct process for students, the teacher makes the instructional decision to incorrectly perform the skill to turn the learning process into more of a conversation. After incorrectly serving the ball, the following conversation might occur.

Teacher: What feedback do you have for me after analyzing my form?

Student 1: I think you may need to hold the ball lower before you strike it.

Teacher: I like that. Turn and talk to your neighbor—why is this important?

(Students briefly discuss with their partners. The teacher invites them to offer more feedback.)

Student 1: I saw you toss the ball before you hit it. That is making you not have a lot of control of the ball.

Student 2: I agree. I think the ball will go over the net more often if you held it steady before hitting it.

Teacher: Thanks for that feedback. I'll use it and try again. Keep an eye on my form this time.

(Teacher serves the ball again.)

Student 3: That time, you stepped with the same foot that you hit the ball with.

Teacher: Why is that a problem since the ball went over the net?

Student 3: I actually don't know why.

Student 4: Stepping with your opposite leg allows you to stay balanced.

Teacher: Thanks for that feedback. Let me use that and serve the ball one more time. Keep an eye on my form again.

(Teacher serves the ball again.)

After this last serve, the students do not have additional feedback to offer. She directs students to go to their groups, where they will have two group members serve while the others provide feedback in the same manner.

After a few minutes of practice, the teacher asks the class to come back as a whole group to clarify what they are looking for in a quality serve. Students respond with many answers, such as stepping with the opposite foot of the serving arm, doing a pendulum swing, striking the ball with the wrist, keeping the body and ball low, not tossing the ball before striking it, and having a good follow-through, and the teacher writes down those criteria for them to follow in their group work. Once students are doing peer assessment in their groups, the teacher takes on more of a coaching role, walking around and finding moments where she may need to provide additional feedback. However, most of the work from instruction to assessment now lies in the hands of the learners.

Note how the teacher embeds the following components of cooperative learning into her instructional process.

- **Questioning:** The teacher asks not only for suggestions but also for reasons why those suggestions are important to produce a quality serve.

- **Modeling:** The teacher starts with a low-quality serve but ends the lesson modeling all the components necessary for a quality serve. Not only does she model it, but students also generate a list of success criteria for group work and peer assessment.

- **Productive failure:** The teacher does not start out the lesson with a perfect serve. She makes mistakes, takes advice, asks for feedback, and acts on the feedback she receives. She is vulnerable throughout the process and allows feedback to improve her practice. She outlines why that feedback is important.

In another case, imagine a world language teacher working with his novice language learners on writing an example high-quality paragraph. At the end of the unit, individual students will write a description about themselves and others for their summative assessment. For this instructional activity, which the teacher has planned for midway through the unit, the class as a whole will develop an exemplar describing a classmate that they imagine. The teacher gives the students several minutes to talk in small groups about what elements will need to be present to model proficiency and then brings the class together to write the exemplar. The students give their imaginary classmate a name and then proceed to collaborate and provide a description of this person. The teacher serves as the scribe and collects the students' thoughts on the front board or screen so everyone can follow along and provide feedback. Individual students add sentences or corrections along the way until they are satisfied with the product. Once the students have produced a writing sample, the students analyze it for quality using a rubric that the teacher provided at the outset of the unit. This is the same rubric that will be used for the summative assessment. They can then make any additional changes until they feel that the exemplar is a good representation of proficiency with the skills they are developing. This activity is a powerful way to involve students in practicing their skills and provides multiple opportunities for the students and teacher to assess sample work in a low-risk environment.

Strategic Grouping

The cycle of effective assessment practices often comes back to deciding how to target intervention and enrichment to meet the needs of a diverse group of students. Teachers must carefully consider their choices of how to group students during instruction and practice, whether those be heterogeneous (a diverse group of students with varying readiness levels) or homogeneous (a teacher-selected group of students based on similar readiness levels), to ensure that proficiency advances throughout the learning experiences. With strategic groupings, instead of reteaching a concept to a whole class, teachers can pinpoint instruction for the specific students who need additional support. Conversely, students who need enrichment can have their own space to explore, wonder, and dive deeper into the content. This requires teacher reflection, intentionality, and a commitment to allow personalization in the learning process.

When grouping students, teachers must consider their own availability and readiness to offer support. For example, when grouping students with the same misconception, teachers must be readily available for reteaching, or they must design activities to ensure that groups of students do not continue to practice incorrectly. Teachers must think about how each group's members will engage with the content in a way that advances their proficiency while not necessarily having the immediate availability of the teacher. When creating groups for intervention or enrichment, or just for a warm-up activity, consider using the structure provided in figure 6.2 to ensure that students are targeting skills; the teacher, or someone with a proficient understanding, is available to help coach; and there is a way to confirm that learning has occurred.

Group 1	Group 2	Group 3	Group 4
Group members:	Group members:	Group members:	Group members:
Targeted skill:	Targeted skill:	Targeted skill:	Targeted skill:
Teacher role:	Teacher role:	Teacher role:	Teacher role:
I will check for understanding by:	I will check for understanding by:	I will check for understanding by:	I will check for understanding by:

FIGURE 6.2: Collaborative group planning template.

*Visit **go.SolutionTree.com/assessment** for a free reproducible version of this figure.*

Common practice when creating groups with varying readiness or skill levels is to place one student with a greater understanding in a group to provide coaching and support for students who struggle. If students who receive this responsibility do not have a masterful understanding of the target, they may offer misguided or even incorrect advice and support; their guidance may not be as reliable, since teachers' content expertise exceeds that of the students. That said, the role of the teacher, even in these groupings, is critical. When teachers are confident about student proficiency levels, they know more about when to provide additional support or when to step back and observe. Thus, the decision about pairings and groupings is nuanced and requires great thought about what is the most productive configuration.

Realizing the Advantages of a Student-Centered Experience

Students are the ones who are doing the learning, so it is essential that they are at the center of all instructional decisions. Assessment and instruction must not only gauge understanding to allow for agility but also embrace mistakes as a natural part of learning. In the following sections, we will explore the power of failure and creating a fluid assessment and instruction cycle.

The Power of Failure

Failure, and how one responds to failure, is an important part of learning. Carol S. Dweck (2006, 2016) points out that the reaction to those moments of failure is what determines whether a student has a fixed or growth mindset. According to Dweck (2016):

> Believing that your qualities are carved in stone—the *fixed mindset*—creates an urgency to prove yourself over and over. If you have only a certain amount of intelligence, a certain personality, and a certain moral character—well, then you'd better prove that you have a healthy dose of them. It simply wouldn't do to look or feel deficient in these most basic characteristics. (p. 6)

With this understanding, if the primary purpose of instruction is to teach and the primary purpose of assessment is to score, students will not learn how to re-engage with content when setbacks occur. They may view feedback as something that is done to them, instead of a conversation that allows them to partner with the teacher. Students may see wrong answers as failures, instead of opportunities to learn. Learning is an active process for students, and instruction should carefully consider how failure and the teacher's response to it are part of daily instruction.

Alternately, Dweck (2016) explains:

> This *growth mindset* is based on the belief that your basic qualities are things you can cultivate through your efforts, your strategies, and help from others. Although people may differ in every which way—in their initial talents and

aptitudes, interests, or temperaments—everyone can change and grow through application and experience. (p. 7)

With this understanding, we must question our current practices to answer the questions, Do we use assessment (as a noun) as an opportunity to quantify learning? Or, do we assess (as a verb) alongside instruction to fill deficits and encourage learners to re-engage with the material in a way that improves their understanding? Effective assessment promotes strong instruction as students learn the power of reflection, engagement, and increased learning. Teachers can intentionally help students develop a growth mindset by carefully considering how to deliver the content, engaging the students with the content, and coaching the students in safe and authentic ways that advance their proficiency.

The purpose of practice is to improve, and assessment is intentional practice paired with evidence-based, targeted feedback. It should be a time when students can learn from their mistakes and reflect on what went well and what needs improvement. In order to promote a growth mindset, consider the following ways that teachers can encourage re-engagement and productive responses to moments of failure.

- **Encourage reflection on feedback:** After providing feedback on assessments, build five to ten minutes into the next class period for reflection and resubmission. Protect this time, and allow students a chance to talk, share, and continue the learning process.

- **Look for ways to be collaborative:** Repurpose some assessments that used to be obtrusive as unobtrusive, collaborative group experiences. During these events, walk around, not judging correctness but looking for immediate opportunities to coach and provide feedback. This way, students are getting the same experiences, but the collaboration promotes increased engagement and opens the door for classroom conversations of reflection and learning.

- **Be vulnerable and share your mistakes:** As learners often view teachers as the content experts, they must understand that their teachers also make errors. Embrace mistakes and show students how you learn from them. Intentionally display incorrect answers, and allow students to provide feedback.

- **Never put a stop to learning:** Allowing reassessment communicates to students that learning does not have a deadline. Encourage students to keep going, even if a summative event has occurred.

- **Look for patterns in student mistakes:** By explicitly addressing common mistakes, you can normalize errors and focus your instruction on responding to these errors when they occur.

- **Ask students to share their "best" mistakes:** Through instruction, teachers can mindfully ask students to share mistakes that they made and how they responded. This opens the door to talk about failure and respond productively.

If teachers want students to develop a growth mindset and learn to deal with failure, they must address it through the instructional process. Many traditional instructional, assessment, and grading practices have normalized penalizing mistakes, even early in the learning process when teachers do not yet expect proficiency, leading to a fixed mindset in students. Normalizing errors and focusing on how students will respond will help change mindsets. In the end, productive failure promotes increased learning.

A Fluid Cycle

A student-centered, productive learning experience is created through the fluid cycle of assessment, instruction, and feedback. This cycle has no ending point; students and teachers are learning throughout the entire iterative process. Students are at the heart of this cycle, as teachers make all decisions with students' best interests in mind. If any part of this cycle is missing, the student-centered learning experience is shattered. Figure 6.3 provides a visualization of this cycle.

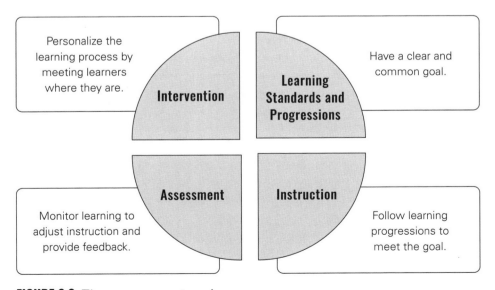

FIGURE 6.3: The assessment cycle.

Instruction is most effective when this cycle is complete and whole. Learning standards and progressions provide consistency either within teams or through vertical articulation of standards within a school. This piece ensures that there are accurate inferences and interpretations of the standards and that proficiency looks the same from class to class and teacher to teacher. This is non-negotiable and needs to be set in stone before starting a new unit to ensure that instruction is effective.

Some teachers may fear that with a student-centered learning experience comes an end to direct instruction. In many courses, teachers cannot teach standards without the direct instruction component, and this practice should not end. Teachers are the content experts, and they will many times need to explicitly teach new content to learners in a direct fashion. There are moments when direct instruction is the most effective and appropriate mode of delivery, but teachers can make these experiences more student centered by determining when assessment is most appropriate to respond to students' needs. Teachers can seamlessly infuse many unobtrusive assessment strategies from chapter 4 (page 73) into predesigned instruction to ensure that they are meeting student needs. In this manner, the instruction is still direct but works alongside assessment so that the teacher is constantly observing and modifying. With sound assessment practices, instruction is no longer a matter of deliver and score, but that fluid cycle of deliver, observe, and respond. Using assessment as a learning experience involves guiding students through new learning, and instruction supports that mission.

Learning for Teachers

Teachers can render a well-structured lesson plan meaningless if instructional agility and infused assessment do not play a central role in the learning process. Instruction benefits the teacher as much as the student; the intentionality of the design is what makes instruction a learning experience. For example, a common practice allowing for gradual release of responsibility (Pearson & Gallagher, 1983) when it comes to instruction is the *I do, we do, you do* method. Through this method, the teacher can model first; then the teacher and students can collaborate through the process before the teacher turns learning over to the students (Fisher & Frey, 2008, 2014). To incorporate more assessment into instruction and allow for increased learning on the part of the teacher, teachers can turn the three stages into four by incorporating *you collaborate* before the *you do* stage. This still puts learning and practicing into the hands of students but infuses an intentional assessment check to ensure students are ready to work independently. *You collaborate* incorporates discussion and teamwork, allowing the teacher to circulate, collect informal formative data, and respond appropriately. In this collaborative stage, the teacher can make several instructional decisions to personalize the learning process, such as deciding a certain student needs more individual instruction, another student needs a challenge, or all the students must regroup for more whole-class instruction.

Teachers should leave a lesson knowing more about their learners than when they entered the lesson. Through instruction, teachers should be constantly learning about:

- Emerging individual, small-group, or whole-class needs

- How students react when they are frustrated or confused

- How students act when they are bored or disengaged

- How students respond to coaching and feedback

Outside of delivering content, instruction is a time to actively learn more about the students in the classroom. Observation and conversation are an essential part of daily instruction that teachers should use to increase their knowledge of students.

Learning for Students

Instruction is the union of teaching content, providing feedback, responding to student needs, infusing ongoing assessment, and ensuring that students react to feedback and re-engage with the content. Ultimately, a culture of learning places the *student* at the center of the learning and assessment experience. With that said, teachers do not need to be the only people in charge of assessment, feedback, and next steps. Consider giving students a list of learning targets such as the one in figure 6.4.

On the first day of the unit, the teacher can use this list as a preassessment tool. The teacher introduces students to the targets and asks them to check off the skills they are familiar or proficient with upon entering the unit in the Check-In 1 column. After a few days of learning and the incorporation of assessment and feedback, the learners once again engage with the learning targets in the Check-In 2 column. This time, the teacher asks them to engage to a greater extent by doing the following with partners at their table.

1. Find one check mark that you didn't have the last time, and share with your table partners what you didn't understand about the learning target the first time around.

2. Identify one target that does not have a check mark, and ask your table partners a question. (If all targets are checked, ask a question that you feel others might struggle with.)

3. At the bottom of your checklist, write a question for the teacher.

Standard: Understand the concept of a unit rate a/b associated with a ratio $a{:}b$ with $b \neq 0$, and use rate language in the context of a ratio relationship. (6.RP.A.2)				
Learning Targets	Check-In 1	Check-In 2	Check-In 3	Check-In 4
I can explain the concept of a ratio.				
I can explain the concept of unit rate.				
I can identify unit rate from a story.				
I can identify unit rate from a table.				
Questions for Teacher:				

Source for standard: NGA & CCSSO, 2010b.

FIGURE 6.4: Student self-assessment check-in template.

*Visit **go.SolutionTree.com/assessment** for a free reproducible version of this figure.*

During this time, the teacher has the opportunity to walk around and listen to students engage in conversation about their understanding. This formative opportunity is part of the instructional process, but strategically designed to put the learning in students' hands. Additionally, adding a question to the bottom of the checklist promotes self-advocacy and allows the teacher to get to know each student's needs to begin planning for the next instructional experience. If one student expresses extreme frustration or confusion, the teacher can plan individual conferencing. If several students express concern with, for example, finding unit rate from a table, the teacher can use modeling and prompts during a guided demonstration the next day. The teacher can also create strategic groupings for the following day's activities.

According to John Hattie's (2009) research, "Students have a reasonably accurate understanding of their levels of achievement" (p. 43). Thus, students have a very high ability to predict their own achievement. Inviting them to engage in these metacognitive practices allows them the time to learn about themselves and share what they need when it comes to extending their learning. It also allows the teacher to gain insight into their reflections and feelings.

When collaborative teams meet to plan and discuss instruction, the three big ideas and the four critical questions of a PLC are essential supports.

Collaboration Around Assessment

Sound instruction ensures that there is a focus on learning and results. When teachers collaborate on instruction, they collectively coach students through the acquisition of new knowledge while personalizing the learning process to place the primary focus on increased learning. The results from instruction may come in the form of increased engagement, more self-confidence, and an understanding of how to self-advocate. Collaboration takes place in the form of sharing resources and expertise with the primary goal of meeting students where they are. Collaborative teams, especially those that work within a PLC, bring minds together for a common goal to enhance students' learning experience.

Since instruction brings the assessment process full circle, teams address all four critical questions of a PLC (DuFour et al., 2016). When teams are designing cohesive instruction, the four critical questions must be at the forefront of thinking and planning.

When designing instruction, collaborative teams must address the question of what students need to know and be able to do first. The shared understanding of standards and targets is the foundation for teachers to design effective instruction. This foundation ensures that when they design instruction, they are hitting the appropriate level of rigor. Pacing guides or shared calendars are helpful and transition easily to the incorporation of common assessment.

To find out when students have learned it, teachers embed both formal and informal assessment into daily plans and activities. If teachers hope to hit the target, they need data that support their assumptions and guide instruction. Collaborative teams can make instructional decisions to intentionally plan common assessments and discuss the data.

Questions 3 and 4 (What will we do when they haven't learned it? and What will we do when they already know it?; DuFour et al., 2016) help teams focus their efforts toward intervention and enrichment. While collaborative teams strategically design assessment, the intervention and enrichment at the classroom level should be as unique as the learners within that class. With instruction, it is challenging to plan precisely what the day-to-day experiences look like because of the diversity present within classrooms. For teams, the focus for questions 3 and 4 lies in curating a wide range of resources and strategies to answer these questions. Whether the intervention (at the classroom level) is reading questions to a student, reteaching using manipulatives, modeling and having students repeat, incorporating a new graphic organizer, providing an extension prompt, or chunking content, what is important is that the intervention matches the needs of the learner. With these resources, classroom teachers have a bank to pull from when a learner needs intervention or enrichment. Teams may choose to use a tool such as the one in figure 6.5 to ensure that through instruction, teachers can access a resource that provides guidance on timing, possible questions to ask to gauge proficiency, assessments available to them, and resources designed for intervention and enrichment.

Standard:				
Learning Target	Questions to Check for Proficiency	Timing	Assessment	Resources

FIGURE 6.5: Aligned resources planning template.

*Visit **go.SolutionTree.com/assessment** for a free reproducible version of this figure.*

With shared tools such as this, teachers within a collaborative team can constantly add to and strengthen the resources available to their team.

Questions for *Reflection*

*Use these questions to reflect on this chapter's
learning and begin to look forward.*

1. In our classrooms or school, do both teachers and students view
    assessment as a supportive process?

2. In the assessment cycle, what is an area that our team
    can improve on?

3. How have we used questioning or guided instruction to
    support student learning?

4. How do we inspire continued learning and growth in students
    through setbacks or perceived failure?

5. What steps have we or our school taken to create a culture of
    learning and place the learner at the center of the learning and
    assessment experience?

6. When it comes to assessment, what is the next step for our
    team? How do we hope to accomplish that goal?

Next Steps for Planning Daily Instruction

Clearly understand and engage with the standards and learning progressions to design cohesive instruction.

Check lesson plans to ensure that unobtrusive, informal assessment is embedded into every lesson.

Ensure through the lesson plans that each lesson can answer the question, Did they learn it?

Ensure that lessons have an effective marriage of alignment, instruction, assessment, and intervention.

Remind students to be vulnerable in the assessment process, and use the feedback loop to keep students involved.

Conclusion

Gone are the days of teach, assess, and then hope for the best. As an educational community, we have learned so much about the assessment process that we have a moral imperative to continue our learning and implementation of high-quality assessment practices. In order for students to view assessment as a means by which to learn rather than a means by which to be judged, teachers must make sure that their own focus is on learning.

When assessment *is* learning, students see assessment as an ongoing process. They do not see assessment as something to fear; rather, they see it as an opportunity to show what they know, understand, and can do. They believe mistakes and errors are part of learning and growth. Students are hopeful and develop self-efficacy. In sum, students know that learning is always on the horizon, and they are confident that they will continue to improve.

When assessment *is* learning, teachers believe that *all* students can and will achieve, and they pass this belief along to students. They model learning-focused language and provide students with multiple opportunities to show their skills in a low-risk environment. This environment supports a classroom and school culture where all learners thrive.

When assessment *is* learning, teachers and collaborative teams approach it as a process by which everyone in the classroom learns. In this book, we have outlined how steps in the assessment process support a student-centered assessment experience focused on progress and achievement. This assessment process uses backward design to give students and teachers clarity on their objectives, an understanding of what proficiency looks or sounds like, insight as to how students will show their learning, and transparent alignment with daily instruction and classroom activities. Now that you have had a chance to read about each step of this responsive and fluid process of assessment, take another look at the whole process; figure C.1 (page 134) reviews the cycle that you first saw in the introduction of this book (page 1).

Step 1	Identify priority standards.
Step 2	Develop learning progressions.
Step 3	Determine summative assessment tools.
Step 4	Determine formative assessment tools (both formal and informal).
Step 5	Plan for daily instruction.

FIGURE C.1: Assessment process.

Creating a positive environment through high-quality assessment practices will ensure learning for both students and teachers. Teachers and collaborative teams that focus on learning, results, and collaboration through assessment share the heavy lifting of this work and curate a powerful bank of ideas for how they can improve students' achievement and learning experiences. Assessment is an all-hands-on-deck endeavor to support growth for *all* students. Schools and classrooms are communities of learning that embrace assessment as an integral part of teaching.

Assessment *is* a catalyst for learning.

References and Resources

Ainsworth, L. (2013). *Prioritizing the Common Core: Identifying specific standards to emphasize the most.* Englewood, CO: Lead + Learn Press.

American Council on the Teaching of Foreign Languages. (n.d.). *World-Readiness Standards for Learning Languages.* Accessed at www.actfl.org/sites/default/files /publications/standards/World-ReadinessStandardsforLearningLanguages.pdf on November 29, 2020.

American Council on the Teaching of Foreign Languages. (2017). *NCSSFL-ACTFL can-do statements: Proficiency benchmarks.* Accessed at www.actfl.org/sites/default/files/can -dos/Novice%20Can-Do_Statements.pdf on April 6, 2021.

Aronson, E. (1978). *The jigsaw classroom.* Thousand Oaks, CA: SAGE.

Bangert-Drowns, R. L., Kulik, J. A., & Kulik, C.-L. C. (1991). Effects of frequent classroom testing. *Journal of Educational Research, 85*(2), 89–99.

Beaumont, C., O'Doherty, M., & Shannon, L. (2011). Reconceptualising assessment feedback: A key to improving student learning? *Studies in Higher Education, 36*(6), 671–687.

Black, P., Harrison, C., Lee, C., Marshall, B., & Wiliam, D. (2003). *Assessment for learning: Putting it into practice.* Buckingham, UK: Open University Press.

Black, P., & Wiliam, D. (1998a). Assessment and classroom learning. *Assessment in Education: Principles, Policy and Practice, 5*(1), 7–74.

Black, P., & Wiliam, D. (1998b). *Inside the black box: Raising standards through classroom assessment.* London: School of Education, King's College London.

Black, P., & Wiliam, D. (2010). Inside the black box: Raising standards through classroom assessment. *Phi Delta Kappan, 92*(1), 81–90.

Bransford, J. D., Brown, A. L., & Cocking, R. R. (Eds.). (2000). *How people learn: Brain, mind, experience, and school* (Expanded ed.). Washington, DC: National Academies Press.

Brookhart, S. M. (2013). Classroom assessment in the context of motivation theory and research. In J. H. McMillan (Ed.), *SAGE handbook of research on classroom assessment* (pp. 35–54). Thousand Oaks, CA: SAGE.

Chappuis, J. (2015). *Seven strategies of assessment for learning* (2nd ed.). Boston: Pearson.

Chappuis, J., & Stiggins, R. (2020). *Classroom assessment for student learning: Doing it right—using it well* (3rd ed.). New York: Pearson.

Chappuis, J., Stiggins, R., Chappuis, S., & Arter, J. (2012). *Classroom assessment for student learning: Doing it right—using it well* (2nd ed.). Boston: Pearson.

Chappuis, S., Commodore, C., & Stiggins, R. (2017). *Balanced assessment systems: Leadership, quality, and the role of classroom assessment.* Thousand Oaks, CA: Corwin Press.

Chappuis, S., Stiggins, R., Arter, J., & Chappuis, J. (2004). *Assessment for learning: An action guide for school leaders.* Portland, OR: Pearson Assessment Training Institute.

Cowan, J. (1998). *On becoming an innovative university teacher: Reflection in action.* Buckingham, UK: Society for Research into Higher Education & Open University Press.

Cowan, J. (2006). *On becoming an innovative university teacher: Reflection in action* (2nd ed.). Buckingham, UK: Society for Research into Higher Education & Open University Press.

Dean, C. B., Hubbell, E. R., Pitler, H., & Stone, B. J. (2012). *Classroom instruction that works: Research-based strategies for increasing student achievement* (2nd ed.). Alexandria, VA: Association for Supervision and Curriculum Development.

Dimich, N. (2015). *Design in five: Essential phases to create engaging assessment practice.* Bloomington, IN: Solution Tree Press.

DuFour, R., & DuFour, R. (2012). *The school leader's guide to Professional Learning Communities at Work.* Bloomington, IN: Solution Tree Press.

DuFour, R., DuFour, R., Eaker, R., & Many, T. (2010). *Learning by doing: A handbook for Professional Learning Communities at Work* (2nd ed.). Bloomington, IN: Solution Tree Press.

DuFour, R., DuFour, R., Eaker, R., Many, T. W., & Mattos, M. (2016). *Learning by doing: A handbook for Professional Learning Communities at Work* (3rd ed.). Bloomington, IN: Solution Tree Press.

Dweck, C. S. (2006). *Mindset: The new psychology of success.* New York: Random House.

Dweck, C. S. (2016). *Mindset: The new psychology of success* (Updated ed.). New York: Random House.

Earl, L. M. (2013). *Assessment as learning: Using classroom assessment to maximize student learning* (2nd ed.). Thousand Oaks, CA: Corwin Press.

Erkens, C. (2013, October 27). *Cinderella summatives* [Blog post]. Accessed at www.anamcaraconsulting.com/wordpress/2013/10/27/cinderella-summatives-2 on December 2, 2020.

Erkens, C. (2016). *Collaborative common assessments: Teamwork. Instruction. Results.* Bloomington, IN: Solution Tree Press.

Erkens, C. (2019). *The handbook for collaborative common assessments: Tools for design, delivery, and data analysis.* Bloomington, IN: Solution Tree Press.

Erkens, C., Schimmer, T., & Dimich, N. (2017). *Essential assessment: Six tenets for bringing hope, efficacy, and achievement to the classroom.* Bloomington, IN: Solution Tree Press.

Erkens, C., Schimmer, T., & Dimich, N. (2018). *Instructional agility: Responding to assessment with real-time decisions.* Bloomington, IN: Solution Tree Press.

Ferriter, W. M. (2020). *The big book of tools for collaborative teams in a PLC at Work.* Bloomington, IN: Solution Tree Press.

Fisher, D., & Frey, N. (2008). *Better learning through structured teaching: A framework for the gradual release of responsibility.* Alexandria, VA: Association for Supervision and Curriculum Development.

Fisher, D., & Frey, N. (2009a). *Background knowledge: The missing piece of the comprehension puzzle.* Portsmouth, NH: Heinemann.

Fisher, D., & Frey, N. (2009b). Feed up, back, forward. *Educational Leadership, 67*(3), 20–25.

Fisher, D., & Frey, N. (2010). *Guided instruction: How to develop confident and successful learners*. Alexandria, VA: Association for Supervision and Curriculum Development.

Fisher, D., & Frey, N. (2014). *Better learning through structured teaching: A framework for the gradual release of responsibility* (2nd ed.). Alexandria, VA: Association for Supervision and Curriculum Development.

Formative. (n.d.). In *Lexico powered by Oxford online dictionary*. Accessed at www.lexico.com /en/definition/formative on March 23, 2021.

Fuchs, L. S., & Fuchs, D. (1986). Effects of systematic formative evaluation: A meta-analysis. *Exceptional Children, 53*(3), 199–208.

Garrison, C., & Ehringhaus, M. (n.d.). *Formative and summative assessments in the classroom*. Accessed at www.amle.org/wp-content/uploads/2020/05/Formative _Assessment_Article_Aug2013.pdf on June 2, 2021.

Griffin, P. (2007). The comfort of competence and the uncertainty of assessment. *Studies in Educational Evaluation, 33*(1), 87–99.

Hattie, J. (2009). *Visible learning: A synthesis of over 800 meta-analyses relating to achievement*. New York: Routledge.

Hattie, J., & Timperley, H. (2007). The power of feedback. *Review of Educational Research, 77*(1), 81–112.

Heritage, M. (2008). *Learning progressions: Supporting instruction and formative assessment*. Washington, DC: Council of Chief State School Officers.

Heritage, M. (2013). Gathering evidence of student understanding. In J. H. McMillan (Ed.), *SAGE handbook of research on classroom assessment* (pp. 179–195). Thousand Oaks, CA: SAGE.

Hillman, G., & Stalets, M. (2019). *Coaching your classroom: How to deliver actionable feedback to students*. Bloomington, IN: Solution Tree Press.

Jung, H., Diefes-Dux, H. A., Horvath, A. K., Rodgers, K. J., & Cardella, M. E. (2015). Characteristics of feedback that influence student confidence and performance during mathematical modeling. *International Journal of Engineering Education, 31*(1A), 42–57.

Kibble, J. D. (2017). Best practices in summative assessment. *Advances in Physiology Education, 41*(1), 110–119.

Lee, J. (2006, April). *Is test-driven external accountability effective? A meta-analysis of the evidence from cross-state casual-comparative and correlational studies.* Paper presented at the annual meeting of the American Educational Research Association, San Francisco, CA.

Literacy Design Collaborative. (2018). *Student work rubric content understanding dimension options for NGSS science: Grades 9–12.* Accessed at https://ldc-production-secure .s3.amazonaws.com/resource_files/files/000/000/432/original/MASTER_Student _Work_Rubric_Content_Understanding_Dimension_Options-for-NGSS_Science _Gr9-12.pdf on November 28, 2020.

Lubbock, J. (2007). *The pleasures of life.* Fairford, England: Echo Library.

Marzano, R. J. (2017). *The new art and science of teaching.* Bloomington, IN: Solution Tree Press.

Marzano, R. J., Pickering, D. J., & Pollock, J. E. (2001). *Classroom instruction that works: Research-based strategies for increasing student achievement.* Alexandria, VA: Association for Supervision and Curriculum Development.

Mattos, M., DuFour, R., DuFour, R., Eaker, R., & Many, T. W. (2016). *Concise answers to frequently asked questions about Professional Learning Communities at Work.* Bloomington, IN: Solution Tree Press.

National Coalition for Core Arts Standards. (2014). *National Core Arts Standards.* Dover, DE: Author. Accessed at www.nationalartsstandards.org on November 20, 2020.

National Council for the Social Studies. (2017). *The College, Career, and Civic Life (C3) Framework for Social Studies State Standards: Guidance for enhancing the rigor of K–12 civics, economics, geography, and history.* Silver Spring, MD: Author. Accessed at www.socialstudies.org/sites/default/files/2017/Jun/c3-framework-for-social -studies-rev0617.pdf on November 29, 2020.

National Governors Association Center for Best Practices & Council of Chief State School Officers. (2010a). *Common Core State Standards for English language arts and literacy in history/social studies, science, and technical subjects.* Washington, DC: Authors. Accessed at www.corestandards.org/assets/CCSSI_ELA%20Standards.pdf on November 29, 2020.

National Governors Association Center for Best Practices & Council of Chief State School Officers. (2010b). *Common Core State Standards for mathematics.* Washington, DC: Authors. Accessed at www.corestandards.org/assets/CCSSI_Math%20Standards.pdf on November 29, 2020.

NGSS Lead States. (2013). *Next Generation Science Standards: For states, by states.* Washington, DC: National Academies Press.

Ontario Ministry of Education. (2010). *Growing success: Assessment, evaluation, and reporting in Ontario schools.* Toronto: Author. Accessed at www.edu.gov.on.ca/eng /policyfunding/growSuccess.pdf on December 2, 2020.

Organisation for Economic Co-operation and Development. (2005). *Formative assessment: Improving learning in secondary classrooms.* Paris: Author.

Pearson, P. D., & Gallagher, M. C. (1983). The instruction of reading comprehension. *Contemporary Educational Psychology, 8*(3), 317–344.

Popham, W. J. (2007). All about accountability / The lowdown on learning progressions. *Educational Leadership, 64*(7), 83–84.

Popham, W. J. (2008). *Transformative assessment.* Alexandria, VA: Association for Supervision and Curriculum Development.

Ruiz-Primo, M. A., & Li, M. (2013). Examining formative feedback in the classroom context: New research perspectives. In J. H. McMillan (Ed.), *SAGE handbook of research on classroom assessment* (pp. 215–232). Thousand Oaks, CA: SAGE.

Sadler, D. R. (1989). Formative assessment and the design of instructional systems. *Instructional Science, 18*(2), 119–144.

Schimmer, T., Hillman, G., & Stalets, M. (2018). *Standards-based learning in action: Moving from theory to practice.* Bloomington, IN: Solution Tree Press.

SHAPE America—Society of Health and Physical Educators. (2013). *National standards for K–12 physical education.* Reston, VA: Author. Accessed at www.shapeamerica.org /standards/pe on November 29, 2020.

Shepard, L. A. (2000). The role of assessment in a learning culture. *Educational Researcher, 29*(7), 4–14.

Slattery, W. (2018, May 7). *A short glossary of assessment terms.* Accessed at https://serc .carleton.edu/introgeo/assessment/glossary.html on March 22, 2021.

Stiggins, R. (1999). Assessment, student confidence, and school success. *Phi Delta Kappan, 81*(3), 191–198.

Stiggins, R., Arter, J., Chappuis, J., & Chappuis, S. (2007). *Classroom assessment for student learning: Doing it right—using it well.* Upper Saddle River, NJ: Pearson Education.

Visible Learning. (n.d.). *Global research database.* Accessed at www.visiblelearningmetax.com /Influences on March 22, 2021.

Washington University in St. Louis. (n.d.). *Benefits of group work.* Accessed at https://ctl .wustl.edu/resources/benefits-of-group-work/ on August 29, 2020.

Webb, N. L. (2002). *Depth-of-Knowledge levels for four content areas.* Accessed at www .maine.gov/doe/sites/maine.gov.doe/files/inline-files/dok.pdf on June 3, 2021.

White, K. (2016). *Observation and assessment: If I saw it, does it count?* Accessed at https:// allthingsassessment.info/2016/09/09/observation-and-assessment-if-i-saw-it-does-it -count/ on April 16, 2021.

White, K. (2017). *Softening the edges: Assessment practices that honor K–12 teachers and learners.* Bloomington, IN: Solution Tree Press.

Wiggins, G., & McTighe, J. (1998). *Understanding by design.* Alexandria, VA: Association for Supervision and Curriculum Development.

Wiggins, G., & McTighe, J. (2005). *Understanding by design* (Expanded 2nd ed.). Alexandria, VA: Association for Supervision and Curriculum Development.

Wiliam, D. (2013). Feedback and instructional correctives. In J. H. McMillan (Ed.), *SAGE handbook of research on classroom assessment* (pp. 197–214). Thousand Oaks, CA: SAGE.

Wiliam, D. (2018). *Embedded formative assessment* (2nd ed.). Bloomington, IN: Solution Tree Press.

Wormeli, R. (2018). *Fair isn't always equal: Assessment and grading in the differentiated classroom* (2nd ed.). Portland, ME: Stenhouse.

Index

Coaching Your Classroom
Garnet Hillman and Mandy Stalets
In *Coaching Your Classroom*, the authors share a fresh perspective on classroom feedback for all grade levels and content areas. Explore the parallels between classroom teaching and athletic coaching, and learn how to employ specific coaching techniques to create a student-centered culture in your classroom.
BKF845

Standards-Based Learning in Action
Tom Schimmer, Garnet Hillman, and Mandy Stalets
Get past the knowing-doing gap and confidently implement standards-based learning in your classroom, school, or district. Each chapter offers readers a well-thought-out action plan for implementation and effective communication strategies for getting student and parent buy-in.
BKF782

Instructional Agility
Cassandra Erkens, Tom Schimmer, and Nicole Dimich
This highly practical resource empowers readers to become instructionally agile—moving seamlessly among instruction, formative assessment, and feedback—to enhance student engagement, proficiency, and ownership of learning. Each chapter concludes with reflection questions that assist readers in determining next steps.
BKF764

Essential Assessment
Cassandra Erkens, Tom Schimmer, and Nicole Dimich
Discover how to use the power of assessment to instill hope, efficacy, and achievement in your students. Explore six essential tenets of assessment that will help deepen your understanding of assessment to not only meet standards but also enhance students' academic success.
BKF752

Solution Tree | Press *a division of* ▲ Solution Tree

Visit SolutionTree.com or call 800.733.6786 to order.